Japanese Sashiko Inspirations

Susan Briscoe

D&C
David and Charles

For Chie and Reiko

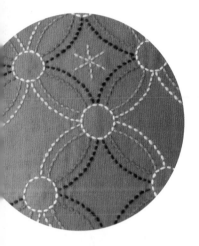

A DAVID & CHARLES BOOK
Copyright © David & Charles Limited 2008
David & Charles is an F+W Publications Inc. company
4700 East Galbraith Road
Cincinnati, OH 45236

First published in the UK in 2008

Text and designs copyright © Susan Briscoe 2008
Illustrations, photography and layout copyright © David & Charles 2008

A catalogue record for this book is available from the British Library.

ISBN-13: 978-0-7153-2641-1 paperback
ISBN-1: 0-7153-2641-4 paperback

Printed in China by SNP Leefung
for David & Charles
Brunel House   Newton Abbot   Devon

Executive Editor   Cheryl Brown
Desk Editor   Bethany Dymond
Project Editor   Lin Clements
Art Editor   Martin Smith
Production Controller   Kelly Smith
Phototography   Kim Sayer, Karl Adamson

Visit our website at www.davidandcharles.co.uk

David & Charles books are available from all good bookshops; alternatively you can contact our Orderline on 0870 9908222 or write to us at FREEPOST EX2 110, D&C Direct, Newton Abbot, TQ12 4ZZ (no stamp required UK only); US customers call 800-289-0963 and Canadian customers call 800-840-5220.

Contents

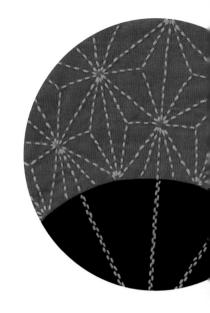

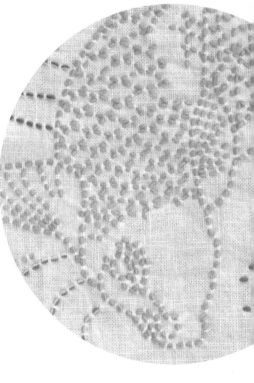

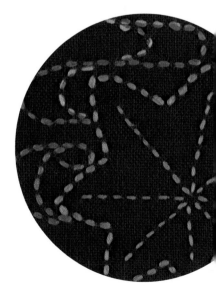

Introduction

Sashiko captures the essence of Japanese design with ease and sophistication, using modern threads and fabrics to create unique works inspired by the rich craft and textile heritage of Japan.

'Traditional' Japanese sashiko conjures up images of white running stitches on indigo, often in intricate traditional patterns. When I began learning sashiko, I wondered why these colours and patterns were used. The women who stitched these designs in the 19th and early 20th centuries used the fabric they had to hand and adapted patterns they saw all around them – perhaps an expensive printed or woven design that took their fancy, stitched in thread specially spun for sashiko. Adapting the design to their own work, inventing a new arrangement of patterns or making something beautiful and necessary for their home were all important skills. But like early quilters, they didn't have the resources that we do and their work was created within these limitations. My sashiko teachers helped me to understand where sashiko patterns and style originated, but also showed me how the tradition was developing today.

Modern quilters and embroiderers have a wealth of colourful threads and fabrics that those early sashiko creators could only dream about. Today we can create gorgeous sashiko that expresses our creativity, while drawing on the kinds of design sources that inspired those earlier stitchers. Our sashiko can be fresh and beautiful, adding a Japanese touch to our homes while complementing our modern lifestyles. The projects in this book explore these possibilities.

Each chapter focuses on a particular set of design inspirations and techniques, centring on a project that combines these in a new and innovative way, while staying true to their oriental origins. A smaller 'taster' project gives the opportunity to try out the technique before beginning the main project. Information about the inspirations and design process is given, to help you go further if you wish and develop your own ideas.

While the look of these sashiko projects is new, the techniques are firmly grounded in the sashiko tradition. This is covered in Getting Started, with everything you need to know about threads, fabrics, marking, stitching and other aspects of sashiko. A brief look at the history of sashiko features traditional pattern adaptation, fabrics and its cultural background, plus a look at some contemporary sashiko in Japan. The Inspiration Gallery beginning on page 120 provides even more ideas for combining sashiko with patchwork, quilting and embroidery.

Have fun and enjoy creating your own sashiko treasures.

Inspirations for Sashiko

Sashiko (meaning 'little stab' or 'little pierce') began as a way to add extra warmth and strength to fabrics, stitched by people living in the north of Japan, where the winters are long and cold. Little early sashiko survives, as it was worn out and used up, but it was probably quite plain. In the last 200 years, sashiko has become more decorative, drawing on the wealth of traditional Japanese design motifs.

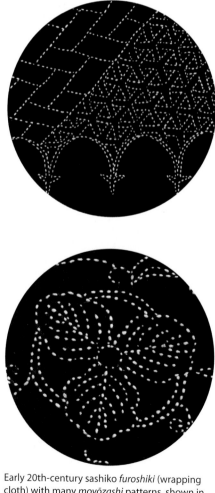

Early 20th-century sashiko *furoshiki* (wrapping cloth) with many *moyōzashi* patterns, shown in detail in the circular pictures.
(Author's collection)

The wives of farmers and fishermen used sashiko to make a variety of garments and household textiles. Specific patterns became linked to different regions while others spread throughout the country, via well-established trade routes. Plain sashiko had no pattern, just simple rows of running stitch, usually through two or more layers of cotton or hemp cloth. The earliest patterned sashiko was probably *hitomezashi* (one-stitch sashiko), imitating the tiny geometric patterns of stencilled *komon* fabric with straight lines of stitches, the patterns appearing where the stitches crossed or met (the Kiku Panel on page 88 explores the potential of several *hitomezashi* designs). Before the Meiji Restoration in 1868, many local sumptuary laws prohibited ordinary people from wearing larger patterns. It is said that *kakurezashi* (hidden sashiko) with indigo on indigo was invented as a way of hiding more elaborate sashiko designs. People were banned from wearing bright colours and were often restricted to indigo fabrics.

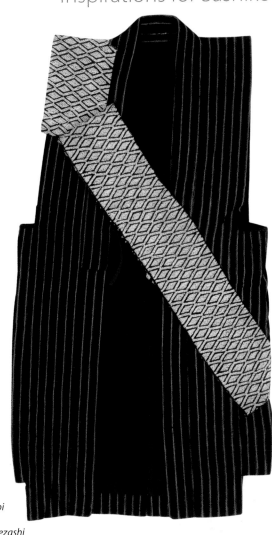

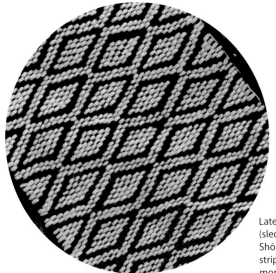

Late 19th-century *sorihikihappi* (sled-hauling waistcoat) from Shōnai, Yamagata, with *hitomezashi* strip for the sled strap (shown in more detail in the circular picture). (Author's collection)

By 1900, cotton had become the most popular cloth for working clothes and large quantities were imported from the USA. It was stronger and more comfortable to wear than many local plant fibres, and even the poor could afford cotton secondhand. Fashions were changing and large-scale patterns were becoming popular for silk kimono. This change in the scale of patterns and the available materials seems to coincide with sashiko's creative flourishing in the early 20th century.

Blank trade flyer (*hikifuda*) showing two women discussing a length of fabric, with a view of an indigo dye works in the lower right corner, c.1910. *Hikifuda* were overprinted by businesses and used for advertising. (Author's collection)

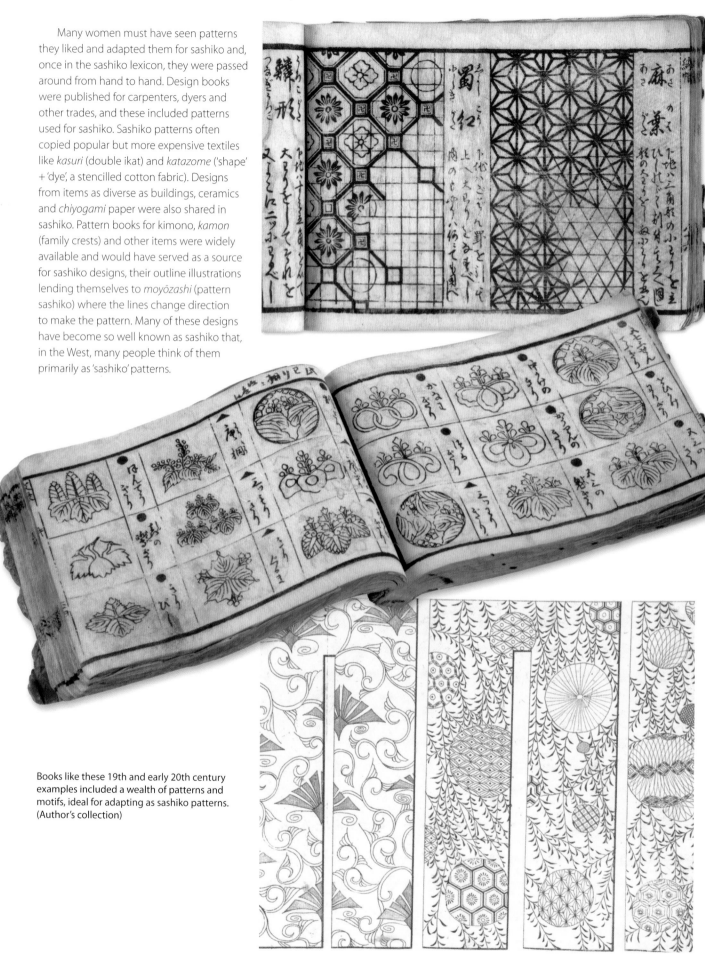

Inspirations for Sashiko

Many women must have seen patterns they liked and adapted them for sashiko and, once in the sashiko lexicon, they were passed around from hand to hand. Design books were published for carpenters, dyers and other trades, and these included patterns used for sashiko. Sashiko patterns often copied popular but more expensive textiles like *kasuri* (double ikat) and *katazome* ('shape' + 'dye', a stencilled cotton fabric). Designs from items as diverse as buildings, ceramics and *chiyogami* paper were also shared in sashiko. Pattern books for kimono, *kamon* (family crests) and other items were widely available and would have served as a source for sashiko designs, their outline illustrations lending themselves to *moyōzashi* (pattern sashiko) where the lines change direction to make the pattern. Many of these designs have become so well known as sashiko that, in the West, many people think of them primarily as 'sashiko' patterns.

Books like these 19th and early 20th century examples included a wealth of patterns and motifs, ideal for adapting as sashiko patterns. (Author's collection)

Inspirations for Sashiko

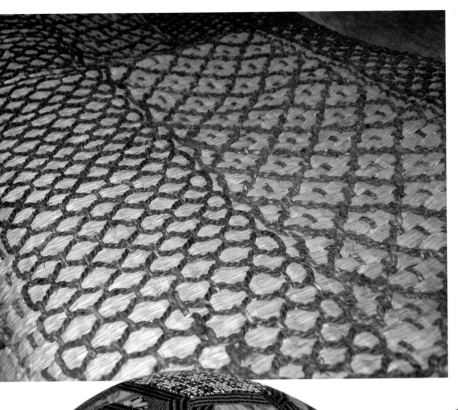

Items made with sashiko show a response to the materials available. Sashiko was stitched on stripes and checks, using the lines in the fabric weave to align the stitches, as in the Sakiori Bolster on page 44. Patchworks of various fabrics were embellished with sashiko, like the Ranru Wall Hanging on page 96. In more prosperous farming areas like Shōnai, Yamagata, sashiko was stitched on the highest quality *kon-iro*, deep blue indigo cotton. Thrifty stitchers backed their work with thin cotton towels and recycled cloth, stitching through both layers, but keeping the best fabric on show.

Rice straw cargo cover for a fishing boat, stitched with the *kikkōzashi* (tortoiseshell stitch) pattern used for the Kiku Panel on page 88. (Aoyama Museum, Yuza-machi)

Modern sashiko stitchers continue the tradition of adapting designs from inspirations they see around them. Many traditional patterns have developed extra variations in sashiko, with double stitching or extra lines in the pattern. More colourful fabrics have superseded indigo for household textiles and sashiko threads and fabrics have kept pace with changing tastes, with shaded threads and 'antique' colours becoming popular, such as those used for the Book Cover Bag on page 58. After a brief decline in the mid 20th century, sashiko has reinvented itself as a craft, combining with patchwork, quilting and appliqué, but constantly finding new inspirations in traditional Japanese design and with new uses for modern lifestyles.

These patchwork balls by Reiko Domon are made from *hitomezashi* samples with patchwork borders – a modern use for traditional sashiko. They are filled with an exercise ball to create the shape.

Getting Started

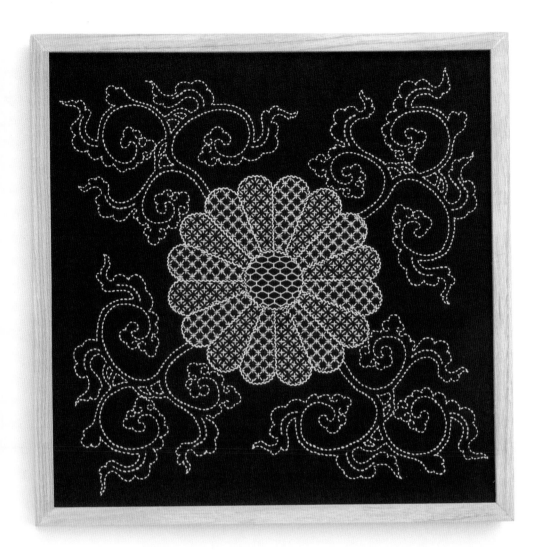

This section contains all the technical information you need to create beautiful sashiko. It will help you choose suitable tools, equipment and materials. The basic information on how to mark the patterns, stitching and finishing your work are all included – essential sashiko know-how at your fingertips.

Tools and Materials

Sashiko requires only basic sewing equipment and materials and you will probably already have a basic sewing kit (see below) which can all be used. Smaller items of equipment are perfect for portable stitching, whether on holiday, in the garden or at a craft group meeting. If you store things together in a neat bag, like the drawstring bag on page 76 or the tote on page 98, you will be ready to go. There's even a needle case on page 46 for your sashiko needles!

Basic equipment

Sewing & Marking Kit

- Sashiko needles (various sizes)
- Sewing needles 'sharps'
- Small embroidery scissors
- Dressmaking scissors
- Pincushion or needle case
- Pins
- Thimble (optional)
- Tacking (basting) thread
- Sewing thread to match your fabrics
- Marking tools (see page 17)
- Rulers – ordinary and quilter's

Marking tools

You will need an assortment of marking tools, including markers for dark and light fabrics, rulers and templates for marking curved designs. Marking tools are described on page 17 and using them on page 21.

Cutting mat and quilter's ruler

These are excellent for precision marking. You might also prefer to cut out your fabrics with a rotary cutter.

Japanese embroidery scissors

Nigiribasami are not essential, but do make sewing sashiko feel very authentic! They are also useful for snipping threads at the sewing machine.

Sewing clamp (*kakehari*)

This sewing clamp (shown below) is sold as a 'third hand' or 'sewing bird'. It is useful for keeping your work under tension when sewing straight lines, but not essential.

Japanese embroidery scissors are useful for snipping thread and certainly look authentic.

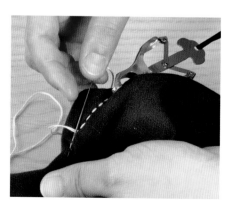

Thimble

Thimbles are optional – use a conventional thimble if you prefer. The traditional Japanese 'ring' thimble is worn on the second joint of the middle finger of your sewing hand with the eye end of a short needle resting against it. The 'coin' thimble, with a dimpled disk to push the needle, is used with longer needles. See Sewing Sashiko (page 25) for more information on sewing technique.

Using a ring thimble.

Using a coin thimble.

Sewing machine

This is useful for assembling projects, although old sashiko items were made completely by hand. Zigzag as well as straight stitching will be useful, as fabrics suitable for sashiko tend to fray and it is a good idea to zigzag the edges before you begin hand stitching, especially with larger projects that will be handled a lot.

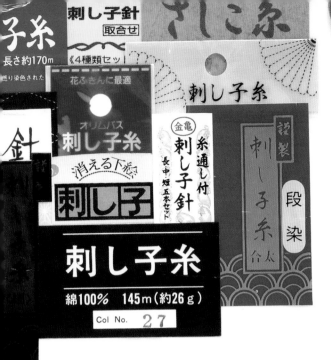

Look for these kanji characters
on Japanese labels, so you know
if the thread is made for sashiko.

刺し子

Thread

Sashiko thread was specially spun, although
ordinary fabric and needles were originally
used. Modern sashiko thread has a looser
twist than many embroidery threads and is
made from long staple cotton. It is therefore
very hardwearing and strong – you can't
snap it! Various brands are sold worldwide,
in large skeins and in several weights – fine,
medium and thick – in a rainbow of colours
and shaded effects as well as white, cream
and indigo. The exact thickness and shade
varies between manufacturers, so use the
same brand throughout a sashiko project.

If you cannot obtain real sashiko
thread, cotton à broder makes a reasonable
substitute. Cotton perlé does not really look
or behave like sashiko thread, although it
can add an interesting colour accent. Thread
made for sashiko will give you the best
results as a beginner and you can experiment
to find other suitable threads later on, once
you know what sashiko thread looks and
feels like. To create additional colours, thread
can be dyed at home, either with natural
or synthetic dyes (see picture overleaf). See
page 22 for using sashiko thread.

Needles

Sashiko needles are, compared with ordinary
Western sewing needles, quite thick and
rigid in relation to their length. They are also
sharp. Very long needles will help keep your
stitching lines straight and speed up your
sewing, once you are used to them. If you
normally hand quilt with 'Betweens' (special
short quilting needles), you may find the
smaller sashiko needles easier to manage at
first, although the smallest are only suitable
for fine sashiko thread. If sashiko needles are
unavailable, try embroidery crewels or larger
darning needles.

Match your sashiko needle to the thread
and fabric weight. Finer threads and smaller
needles will work with slightly heavier fabrics
but it will be difficult to stitch a thick sashiko
thread with a large needle through finer
fabrics (see pictures, left). If sashiko feels like
hard work, change to a finer thread and
needle or to a fabric with a lower thread count.

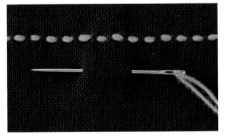

Fine sashiko thread and *tsumugi* cotton fabric
(shown actual size).

Medium sashiko thread and reproduction
sashiko cotton (actual size).

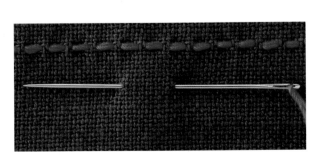

Thick sashiko thread and prairie cloth (actual size).

Some hand-dyed embroidery
threads are suitable for sashiko.

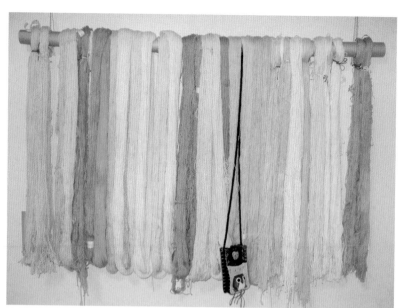

Ready for use in her studio, these sashiko threads were hand dyed with natural materials by Chie Ikeda.

Fabrics

Sashiko was originally stitched on cotton, linen, hemp and other plant fibres. Copies of old hand-woven fabrics are specially made for sashiko, in indigo and other shades (see Suppliers). Fabric and threads often echo natural dyes and 'antique' colours. Choose plain weaves and natural fibres with a lower thread count (the number of threads to the inch), slightly thicker than you might normally choose for quilting. Some quilting and craft fabrics, such as prairie cloth, 'Osnaburg' cloth and cotton flannel, are pleasant to stitch and look authentic. Projects like the Koshi Throw (page 38) and the Sakiori Bolster (page 44) are stitched on stripes and checks, using the weave to line up pattern elements – see cushion, right. Indian cottons made for household textiles are an excellent source of thicker cottons and dressmaking fabrics can be used too. Old sashiko was often stitched on recycled fabrics, so that's another option, but always check that old fabrics are still strong enough to use.

If the fabric is right but you don't like the colour, you can always dye it – imitation indigo dyes (sold for re-dyeing jeans) are easy to use in the washing machine and real indigo home-dyeing kits are available. Internet and mail-order shopping means it is easier than ever to buy materials suitable for sashiko (see Suppliers).

Shown above are three vintage Japanese indigo cottons. . .

. . . followed by five modern Japanese craft cottons. . .

. . . and finally two Indian striped cottons.

Wadding

Sashiko can be stitched through one, two or more layers. Traditionally it was not stitched through quilt wadding (batting) and this can be hard work. Some projects in this book require only one layer, others use two. Butter muslin provides an ideal second layer, as it is soft and easy to stitch through, while having a drape like old multi-layered work. Where wadding is used, I have added it to the project after the sashiko is stitched and additional quilting is sewn parallel to the sashiko. Alternatively, the item can be tied, a method used on old futons and wadded

clothing. I used this method on my Kasuri Throw (page 74). Very thin wadding can be stitched through successfully – look for wadding labelled 'request' weight. Here are some other points on using wadding:

- If you are using dark fabric, remember that the cheaper kinds of white polyester wadding will eventually 'beard' through and spoil your work, so use cotton or blended wadding instead.
- Black wadding is available in dense polyester or cotton and polyester mixtures.

- Cotton wadding can also be dyed dark blue in the washing machine, although it does absorb a lot of dye.
- Old linen blouses, tea towels and flannel sheets can be recycled as wadding/backing, dyed darker as necessary.
- Test a small sample of your chosen wadding/backing combination by stitching a few rows of sashiko – if it is very hard to get the needle through, use thinner wadding or more loosely woven backing fabric.
- Tightly woven calico is not a good choice for backing sashiko!

Fabric markers

Marking your chosen sashiko pattern on the fabric will be easy with the right marker – see page 21 for the various techniques. Marking using Chaco transfer paper is also covered on page 21. Choose a marker you like and marking will be a pleasure.

Hera
The Japanese sewing marker, traditionally made of bone (and now plastic), scores and polishes a line on the cloth. It shows up best on very dark fabrics and the line washes out. Always put a cutting mat or cardboard under your fabric when marking or you will permanently score your table!

Quilter's white pencil
This soft pencil is good for dark fabrics, with marks that wash out or rub off. Sharpen soft pencils with a craft knife, cutting away on either side and trimming to make a flat point – the pencil will last much longer.

Air-erasable marking pen (white)
This is a felt-tip pen that marks white and fades away when exposed to air. The marks only last for 48 hours and can fade sooner, so use it for small projects. Remember to wash out the chemical residue when the work is complete.

White marking pen
This is a roller ball that makes a fine, clear white line which takes a few seconds to 'develop' after drawing. Marks can be removed with water or heat (check individual brand information).

Chaco liner
This Japanese chalk wheel makes marks that brush off easily or wash out. A tiny wheel in the tip picks up chalk and marks the fabric. Chalk refills are available in white, pink, yellow and blue. Use white or yellow on dark fabric.

Chaco pencil
This is a compressed chalk pencil making marks that brush off easily or wash out. Available in the same colours as the Chaco liner. Sharpen the same way as the quilter's white pencil.

Quilter's silver pencil
This is best for light fabrics, as the marks can be difficult to see on dark or medium colours. Marks wash out or rub off. Blue marking pens are another option but must be washed out or the chemicals may damage fabric.

Tailor's chalk
This is an inexpensive marker available in various colours. Marks brush off easily but can be redrawn. It washes out.

Basic Techniques

The basic techniques for sashiko are all here, including drawing and marking patterns, tacking (basting) fabric layers together, starting and finishing work and the sashiko stitching technique.

Imperial or metric?

Patterns can be drawn in imperial or metric measurements. I used imperial for my samples, as the majority of quilters worldwide use this system. Metric equivalents are included for all measurements throughout the book.
1 inch = 2.54 centimetres, so to convert inches to centimetres, multiply by 2.54
1 centimetre = 1.3937 inches, so to convert centimetres to inches, multiply by 1.3937

Neither measurement system is traditional in Japan, where some traditional fabric shops and kimono makers still use the ancient *sun* and *shaku* (Japanese feet and inches) system. If you want to try traditional proportions, one *sun* is made up of ten *bu* and equals 1.193in (3.03cm) and ten *sun* make one *shaku*, 11.93in (30.3cm)! These measures were standardized in 1891 and Japan officially converted to the metric system in 1959. The old ruler, shown life size below, is marked in *bu* and *sun*.

An old Japanese ruler, shown with contemporary imperial and metric rulers.

Drawing geometric patterns using grids

Make geometric sashiko patterns work for you by learning to draw them. Stencils for some sashiko patterns can be bought in quilt shops and although they are easy to use you have to fit your project to the size of the pattern on the stencil, and only the more popular designs are available. Sheets of complete patterns to trace have similar limitations.

By starting to draw each design with a grid, the traditional *moyōzashi* (pattern sashiko) designs can be marked and stitched the size you want. Each project gives the full dimensions for all the patterns but you can easily change the pattern size for decorative effect by drawing larger or smaller starting grids. The basic grid size

I used is given with each project pattern. Some designs can be stitched straight on to the grid, such as *hitomezashi* (one-stitch sashiko) patterns like *komezashi* (rice stitch, page 91), while others need some extra marking, such as *asanoha* (page 98). Refer to the individual project instructions for details of drawing the patterns.

Most *hitomezashi* (one-stitch sashiko) patterns are stitched back and forth on a grid without extra pattern lines, therefore little variation in the grid size is necessary. Fabric with narrow stripes can be stitched with minimal marking and small checks, e.g. ¼in (6mm), can be stitched without any marking at all.

You will need a ruler to draw any pattern. Quilter's rulers are transparent and have extra lines parallel to the edge, so you can easily draw a grid. Some brands have yellow, pink or green as well as black markings which show up well on dark fabrics. An ordinary clear-plastic ruler is fine for pattern-marking methods using graph paper or a cutting mat marked with a grid.

You will also need a selection of curved templates for curved line patterns. You can make your own circle templates with a protractor and some card or template plastic (available from quilting shops). Old thread spools and coins are useful for smaller circle templates. Look out for plastic lids and other recyclable food packaging materials for making templates.

Varying the grids

Many *moyōzashi* (pattern sashiko) designs are based on a square grid while others require a diagonal or triangular grid (see diagram below left). If you look closely at many traditional Japanese designs with diamonds, hexagons or triangles, you will see that they are not drawn on a true isometric 60-degree – the diamonds look slightly wide, the hexagons a bit squashed and the triangles are not really equilateral. To keep this look, start with a rectangular grid on a 2:1 ratio and fill in with diagonal lines (diagram below centre). If you want an isometric grid, perhaps to integrate your sashiko with patchwork hexagons and stars, use isometric graph paper, the 60-degree angle on a quilter's ruler or a 60/30-degree set square to create the grid (diagram below right).

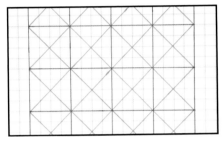

A diagonal or triangular grid.

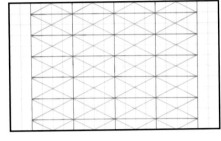

A rectangular grid on a 2:1 ratio.

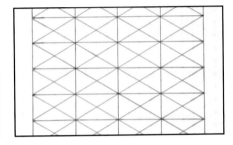

An isometric grid.

Distorting patterns

Grids are also the key to stretching sashiko patterns vertically to give them a different look. Various *moyōzashi* patterns can be treated in this way.

Asanoha is fanned out for the Sensu Tablemat shown here, by drawing the foundation grid following the shape of the fan. The full pattern is given on page 70, so you don't need to distort the pattern yourself. Learn how to mark off a new pattern by drafting the basic design first before embarking on your own distorted version. Patterns like *raimon* (spiral) and *masuzashi* (square measure stitch), where lines are drawn parallel to the outline, are easy to resize or distort – see overleaf for examples. If you enjoy drawing perspective effects other sashiko patterns could be adapted, including more challenging ones with curved lines!

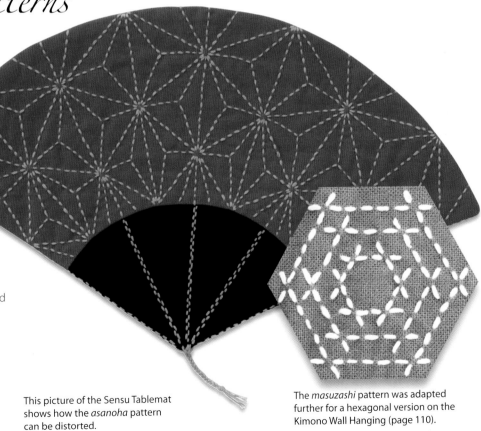

This picture of the Sensu Tablemat shows how the *asanoha* pattern can be distorted.

The *masuzashi* pattern was adapted further for a hexagonal version on the Kimono Wall Hanging (page 110).

19

The Ranru Wall Hanging here has standard and distorted versions of *asanoha* (hemp leaf), *raimon* (spiral) and *masuzashi* (square measure sashiko). These patterns were changed by using the proportions of the outer shape, here a patchwork piece, as a starting point.

Masuzashi as a rectangle

Asanoha repeated twice

Asanoha as a square

Asanoha as a rectangle

Stripes used to line up plain sashiko

Masuzashi as a square

Raimon as a square and then as a rectangle

Transferring ideas – marking methods

There are various methods for marking your sashiko pattern on to your fabric. You can mark the pattern directly on to the top fabric or draw the design on paper and transfer it. Pictorial designs must be traced or photocopied before transferring the pattern.

Marking directly on fabric

This is my favourite method and I use it whenever possible. You can always see exactly what you are marking – nothing hides the fabric! There are many marking materials for dark fabrics (see page 17), so try several and use your favourite. Drawing around curved templates is easier with pencils or pens than with a block of chalk. Some marks stay on the fabric for longer than others but can also depend on things like humidity and hand warmth. If you already have a preferred method for marking dark fabric use that. *Always* follow the manufacturer's instructions when using a new marking product – what removes one kind of mark may permanently set another.

Marking with a quilter's ruler

Quilter's rulers are very accurate. Use the parallel lines on the ruler to mark the base grid for the pattern and mark directly on the fabric. Allow for the width of the line if marking with tailor's chalk – the line can be up to $1/8$in thick, so line up with the bottom of each line or your grid might be $1\frac{1}{8}$in not 1in! Draw the rest of the pattern with curved templates or extra diagonal lines, following individual diagrams in project instructions.

Marking with a cutting mat

Use the grid on a cutting mat to mark the base grid and mark directly on the fabric. Some mats have both imperial and metric grids and you can use an ordinary ruler. The fabric will need to be smaller than the mat, so you can see the mat grid all round the edge, and the ruler should be long enough to reach the opposite sides of the mat. If you don't have a cutting mat, a large sheet of graph paper can be used instead.

Using Chaco paper

Chaco paper is a kind of dressmaker's carbon paper which makes marks that wash out. It can be reused again and again and is available in white, yellow, pink and blue. It is a good method for pictorial designs and motifs, like the Kasuri Throw designs. Not being able to see your fabric while marking can be a disadvantage however – it is just too easy to accidentally move your fabric and spoil the transferred design, so pin the layers together carefully before you start.

Marking a graph with Chaco paper

First draw the pattern on to graph paper. Put the chaco paper face down on the fabric with the pattern on top and pin together. For smaller pieces, just tape the layers to the top of a cutting mat or thick card. Trace along all the design lines with a ballpoint transfer tool – the end of a knitting needle or something similar – making sure you press down well.

A dressmaker's marking wheel can also be used to mark the pattern but the spiked wheel will damage your cutting mat, so use it on some scrap cardboard. When you lift the paper you will see that the pattern has transferred to the cloth. To quickly mark a grid for *hitomezashi*, use a piece of graph paper or squared paper on top and draw along the lines using an ordinary ruler as a guide. When you have finished marking the whole pattern, remove the paper.

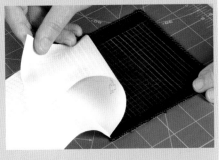

Marking a pictorial motif with Chaco paper

You will find this method useful for the Kiku Panel and the Marumon Screen designs. First copy the picture or motif, by tracing or photocopying the design. The majority of the patterns are given at actual size, so there is no need to resize them (except for the Kasuri Throw). Put the chaco paper face down on the fabric with the pattern on top and pin together. Trace along all the design lines as described above. It is a good idea to use a red ballpoint pen for more complicated pictures, so you can see clearly where you have drawn. Alternatively, trace pictorial motifs using a lightbox, with the pattern under the fabric.

Tacking (basting) fabric layers

Once you have marked your fabric with your sashiko pattern you can prepare the fabric for sewing, if more than one layer is being used. If you are using butter muslin, lay the sashiko fabric right side up on top of the muslin and tack (baste) the layers together vertically and horizontally at approximately 3in (7.6cm) intervals across the panel. In a conventional quilt 'sandwich', the wadding (batting) would go between the top (the sashiko fabric) and the backing (the muslin), before being quilted and bound.

Rather than binding the edges, most projects in this book are 'bagged out', by placing the backing and sashiko right sides together, stitching round the edge and turning the item right side out through a gap left in the stitching. If wadding is added, this means layering the wadding first, then the backing and finally the top, as described in step 4 for the Kasuri Throw (page 78) which is then tied, not quilted. If extra quilting is to be added, as for the Kimono Wall Hanging, the top panel should then by tacked to the backing panel and wadding, tacking near the areas to be quilted, as shown right.

Using sashiko thread

First open out the skein and remove the paper band. Look for the extra loop of thread tied around the skein and cut through all the threads at this point (see picture 1). The threads will seem very long but don't cut them. Sashiko skeins are made to just the right length for using the thread. Hold the other end of the skein and loosely plait the threads to keep them tidy (see picture 2). Draw out individual threads from the top of the plait.

Starting and finishing sashiko stitching

When you have marked your sashiko pattern on your fabric and tacked (basted) the fabric layers together you are ready to begin stitching the sashiko.

The two basic methods of starting are with or without a knot. I almost always choose the knot option as it is so much more secure. Old sashiko garments made from traditional narrow cloth could have the knots hidden in a seam. Sashiko was used for items that received hard wear and the knot-free method can, eventually, come undone.

For either method, first thread your needle with a single length of thread. Pull the two ends together and smooth down the thread to remove any excess twist.

Holding the thread taut between your hands and twanging it with your thumbs is said to get the excess twist out too!

Remember, stitching with doubled thread gives traditional sashiko the 'big stitch' look that is so attractive. It also means that there is no loose end to become frayed and worn during stitching.

Starting and finishing with a knot

Most of the projects use this method. Begin by holding the two ends together and tying an ordinary single knot (sometimes called a quilter's knot). The needle can't escape, very useful if you are sitting on the floor to stitch or working in dim light where lost needles could be trodden on, as in old Japanese farmhouses. Begin stitching with the single knot on the back of your work. The knots don't show on the front. *Hitomezashi* always begins and ends this way, or else it could unravel. When you get to the end, take the needle to the back and wrap the thread around it once. Hold this point between your thumb and forefinger, so the knot can't travel further up the thread, and pull the needle through. If you have left yourself with too little thread to do this, remember you only need about 2.5cm (1in) of thread to tie the knot with the eye end of the needle. This method also uses a *hatamusubi* knot to join in new threads (see overleaf).

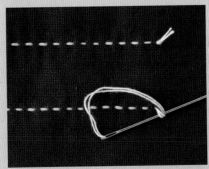

Starting and finishing with a knot (shown from the back of the stitching).

Starting and finishing without a knot

This is possible for *moyōzashi* designs, where the stitches are slightly short but a knot is still the more secure method. No knots are preferable for items that will be seen from both sides, with smaller sashiko stitches.

Start by making several stitches towards the start of the stitch line, going in the opposite direction to your planned stitching, turn around and stitch back over your first stitches, sewing back through the original thread. At the end of the thread, repeat this action in reverse – about ½in–1in (1.3cm–2.5cm) of overlapped stitches is enough. I used a version of this method for the Koshi Throw, pulling a tail of thread through between the top fabric and backing at start and finish.

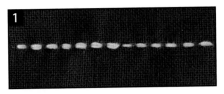

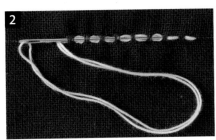

Starting and finishing without a knot (shown from the front of the stitching).

Machine sashiko

Sashiko cannot be stitched by machine. Machine quilting makes a hard, continuous line and the effect of the little running stitches is lost. Even with the imitation hand quilting stitch on many modern high-tech machines, it still doesn't look the same. Some sashiko patterns do make lovely machine quilting designs, especially continuous line patterns like *shippō tsunagi* (page 86), but the finished effect is quite different. The machine lockstitch is akin to couching rather than hand running stitch, which defeats the traditional purpose of sashiko. See also stitch size, overleaf.

Making a *hatamusubi* (loom knot)

In Japan in the past, thread was precious so a *hatamusubi* (joining knot) was used to get the most out of even the last half inch. The harder this knot is pulled, the tighter it becomes. To make tying the knot easier, moisten the ends of the doubled thread so they stick together. The method is the same for right and left-handed people – both hands do equal amounts of work! The secret is in the way the short ends of thread are held whilst the knot is tied. Practise using different coloured threads.

A hatamusubi (loom knot), shown in close detail, being used to join in a new thread.

1 Leave a 1in (2.5cm) tail of old thread loose on the back of work (shown in white). Thread the needle but do not knot the new thread. Lay the end(s) of the new thread (shown in red) against the back of the work.

2 Hold the end of the new thread between the first two fingers of your left hand (at point A). Use your left thumb to bend the tail of the old thread over the new. Put your thumb on the crossed threads to hold them. Keep holding these two points until instructed otherwise.

3 Now the long part of the new thread does most of the work. Loop it to the left, as shown by the arrow. Lift your thumb quickly, pass the thread under it and hold the crossed threads firmly again.

4 Take the long part of the new thread under its own tail and over the old thread. At this point you will see that the new thread has made a loop.

5 Continue to hold the thread at point A. Use your right index finger to bend the old thread through the loop and hold the end between your left thumb and left ring finger at point B. Holding the two short ends so they can't flip out of the knot, use the long new thread to gently pull the knot closed with your right hand.

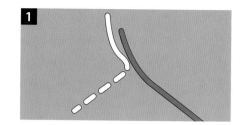

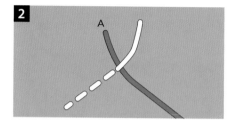

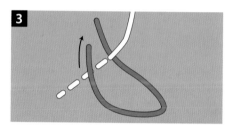

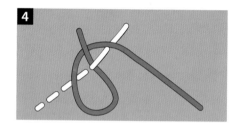

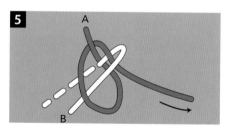

Stitch size

Moyōzashi stitches on old items vary greatly in size, from the tiny stitches on an old *furoshiki* to enormous ones on old rugs. It seems to depend on the number of layers being stitched – more layers mean bigger stitches. Between four and eight stitches to 1in (2.5cm) is about right. Evenness is more important than stitch size. It depends on the thread thickness, number of layers and you!

In *moyōzashi*, the gap between the stitches is about half the length of the stitch. You will be able to count stitches in short sections of the pattern or use

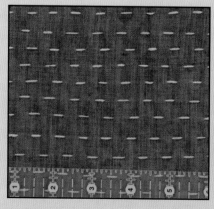

intersecting pattern lines to help gauge your stitches. Like hand quilting, you will find your sashiko settles down to a regular stitch length with practise. *Hitomezashi* stitches relate to the size of the grid.

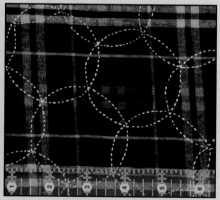

These pictures show different sashiko stitch sizes: large stitches on an old rug (left) and much smaller stitches on an antique *furoshiki* (above).

Sewing sashiko

In Japanese sewing, the needle is held still and the fabric placed on it in a pleating action, several stitches at a time, rather than making individual stitches with the needle being moved through fixed fabric. A quilting frame or hoop is not therefore used for sashiko and it is not stitched from the centre outwards, like Western quilting, but from one side to the other.

The four pictures here show the general sequence to be followed when sewing sashiko.

Begin stitching at one side of the pattern and work your way across. Traditionally, a *kakehari* (third hand or sewing bird – see page 14) is used to hold large pieces of fabric under tension and you might like to try this.

Push the needle through when it is full and smooth the stitches out between your thumb and forefinger, but don't fluff up the thread by scraping it with your nails. This is how to make stitches where the double thread will lie parallel, making patterns appear quite bold and creating a textured effect with the stitches slightly raised.

Taking one stitch at a time will twist the threads and spoil your sashiko, so try to take several stitches whenever possible, even on pictorial designs. You can use a coin thimble (see page 14) to help push the needle through thicker projects or just hold the needle as you would normally – it isn't necessary to hold the needle in the Japanese way to sew good sashiko.

The needle going into the fabric and taking several stitches.

Needle coming out of the fabric.

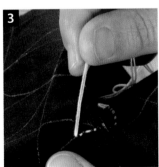
Pulling the thread through and gathering up.

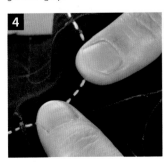
Easing the gathers out.

Sashiko stitching tips

Watch out for the following points when stitching *moyōzashi* designs.

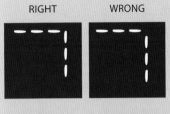

RIGHT   WRONG

- When turning corners, make the last stitch right into the corner so the pattern is sharply defined.

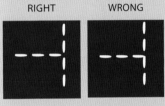

RIGHT   WRONG

- Where pattern lines meet, space the stitches so they don't touch each other.

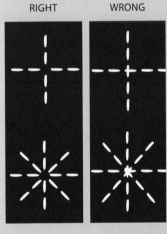

RIGHT   WRONG

- Where pattern lines cross, make a slightly longer gap between stitches, so stitches don't cross on the right side, making an ugly lump (and a weak point). Avoid joining in new threads at these points. In some *hitomezashi* patterns, however, the stitches are supposed to cross.

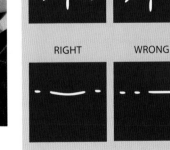

RIGHT   WRONG

- Where indicated in some patterns, you will need to strand loosely across the back of your work. For a quilt where the back will be seen, run the thread between the backing and wadding.

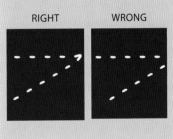

RIGHT   WRONG

- When you make a sharp change of direction, leave a little loop on the back for ease. When stitching *hitomezashi* patterns, take care to always leave turning loops in or your sashiko will pucker up! (see overleaf).

Moyōzashi sashiko patterns

These designs have curved or straight lines of running stitch that change direction to make larger patterns. *Shippō tsunagi* (linked seven treasures), *asanoha* (hemp leaf), *raimon* (lightning spiral) and *masuzashi* (square measure sashiko) are all *moyōzashi* patterns. Pictorial designs, like those on the Kasuri Throw, are also *moyōzashi*.

The two diagrams below illustrate how the project stitch diagrams are constructed. The grids are shown in light blue, the stitching lines in black, the stitching direction in coloured arrows with a coloured dot to show the starting point. Dashed red lines on the diagrams indicate where thread is stranded across the back of the work. The use of circular templates is indicated by tinted circles (usually mauve or pink).

Generally, the diagrams are coloured in this way to assist you with marking and stitching the sashiko.

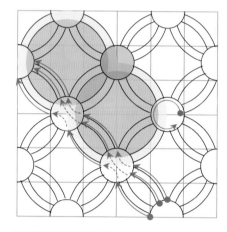

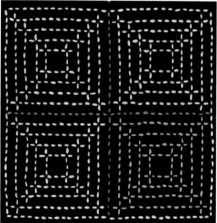

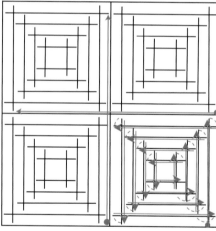

If the grid is also stitched as part of the sashiko pattern, as in this *masuzashi* pattern, then the grid appears as black instead of blue.

Moyōzashi Stitching Tips

- In *moyōzashi*, pattern lines cross but the stitches do not.
- Count the stitches in the short pattern sections for nice, even sashiko.
- When turning corners, make the last stitch right into the corner so the pattern will be sharply defined.
- Where pattern lines meet, space the stitches so they don't touch each other.
- Where indicated in some patterns, strand loosely across the back of your work and when making a sharp change of direction, leave a little loop on the back for ease (see picture, right).

Stranding loosely across the back of the work prevents your sashiko stitches pulling too tightly and distorting the fabric.

Hitomezashi sashiko patterns

Hitomezashi (one-stitch sashiko) designs are worked as a grid of straight lines, where stitches meet or cross to make the design. Most names end with *zashi* (a mutation from *sashi*), which translates best as 'stitch', but all the stitches are really running stitch. Some patterns have vertical and horizontal rows, others have additional diagonal lines while some have horizontal stitches only. *Jūjizashi* is shown right as a stitched sample and as a diagram. For all *hitomezashi*, stitch along the first row, turn your work and stitch back along the next row – first horizontally, then vertically and finally diagonally, as required by the pattern. Additional instructions and information are given with each project.

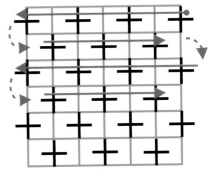

Jūjizashi (shown here) forms the base of several other *hitomezashi* patterns, including *komezashi* and its variations.

Hitomezashi Stitching Tips

- **The grid dictates the stitch size.**
- **Start and finish *hitomezashi* with a simple quilter's knot (see page 23).**
- **Use the *hatamusubi* joining knot to keep thread continuous (see page 24).**
- **Some *hitomezashi* patterns have long threads on the back which are visible on finished items, so you may want to use these for lined projects.**
- **Like all dense stitching, *hitomezashi* will tend to 'pull in' your work more than *moyōzashi* patterns. Leave a loop for ease when turning at the end of each row (see picture right). This is indicated by dashed red lines on diagrams.**

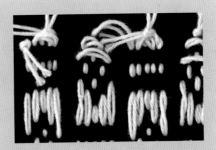

Leave loops at the back of the work (stranding) avoids the stitches pulling the fabric.

Framing

Some of the designs have been made up as wall hangings but they could also be framed. In fact, framing your sashiko is probably the easiest way to finish a panel and make your work look really professional. See right for framing tips.

1 Remove any glass from the frame and the backing panel. Two sides may need trimming down, as the thick sashiko fabric will need to wrap over the edges.

2 Lay the panel right side down on a clean, flat surface and place the backing panel on it centrally. Using a very long length of thread, lace the panel across the back of the frame, horizontally and vertically. You can join on extra thread using the *hatamusubi* knot on page 24. Don't pull the panel too tight.

3 Check the sashiko is square before replacing the board in the frame. If there is glass, clean it so dust is not trapped between the glass and sashiko. Lay the frame flat, put the glass in, then the panel and fold the backing pins back over the panel.

Framing Tips

- **Over time, acid from fibre backing board can damage needlework, so consider placing a sheet of acid-free mounting card between the backing board and the sashiko panel, before you begin lacing.**
- **Keep the sashiko from pressing against the glass with thin strips of mounting card, tucked inside the frame rebate.**
- **If the back of the frame will be visible, such as when you use a screen, cover a thin sheet of card with fabric or printed paper and place it behind the backing board before folding the backing pins in place.**

The Projects

Each of the following projects and smaller 'tasters' include their original design inspirations. These mini projects are just right to experiment with thread, fabric and patterns before embarking on the main project. You can follow the project instructions to the letter or use them as a springboard for your own sashiko creations. Whichever approach you choose, you can explore the wealth of patterns and techniques with pleasure. *Ganbatte kudasai* – work hard!

Mihon Sampler

Samplers have been used to hand down sewing skills all over the world and sashiko is no exception. I find that 4in (10.2cm) squares are ideal for practising new patterns and for small projects, like this elegant sampler table runner. Two *moyōzashi* patterns, both *shippō* (seven treasures) variations, and two *hitomezashi* patterns, *hanabishizashi* (flower diamond stitch) and a *komezashi* (rice stitch) variation plus a *sakura* (cherry blossom) motif complete the sample set. You can try out different thread and fabric combinations on scrap squares left over from other projects. The patchwork format enables you to use your most successful sample squares and favourite patterns, rearranging them until you are happy with the design. If you wish to make it longer you can simply add more sashiko samples.

'Mihon' means 'sample' or 'pattern', and combines the *kanji* characters for 'look' or 'see' and 'book'. This collection of blocks could be the starting point for a more elaborate sampler, using other stitch patterns from this book for extra sashiko squares.

Technique Taster

Customize an album, scrapbook or visitors' book with sampler squares, shaped over card and glued to the cover. Three squares were all I had of the subtle hand-dyed silk noil, but that was all I needed. Perfect for a sashiko project notebook too! See overleaf for instructions.

The Indian cotton stripe border suggested my colour scheme for this table runner, with the shaded pink *sakura* (cherry blossom) echoing the pink line in the stripe for a spring sampler. Suggest another season with a change of stripe and thread colour – there are marumon winter motifs on page 56. See page 35 for runner instructions.

Keepsake Album

Sashiko patterns used: *shippō* (seven treasures) variation, *hanabishizashi* (flower diamond stitch) and *momiji* (maple leaf) motif

Finished size of panels: each 3½in (8.9cm) square

You will need

- Three pieces of silk noil or sashiko fabric, each 4in (10.2cm) square
- Three pieces of thin card, 3½in (8.9cm) square
- Three pieces of thin quilt wadding (batting), 3½in (8.9cm) square
- Medium sashiko thread in light ochre and autumn shades
- Sewing thread
- Basic sewing and marking kit
- Strong PVA adhesive (e.g., woodworking PVA)
- Plain book or album, 8½in x 12in (21.6cm x 30.5cm) (excluding spine) – see Suppliers

Idea

Use just one or two sashiko squares to decorate a smaller book or a box lid. This method also works for scrapbook pages.

Tip

This album project is a great one to use up oddments of thread or to try out new threads – the colours don't have to be the same on each sampler, so experiment.

1 **Marking and stitching:**
Take each 4in (10.2cm) fabric piece and following **Fig 1** and **Fig 2** opposite and **Fig 3** overleaf, mark the patterns as shown (see marking methods, page 21). Stitch the sashiko, following the instructions given with each pattern. Press each finished square.

2 **Assembling the squares:**
Glue a piece of wadding (batting) to each square of card and allow to dry. Place the first sampler square right side down and place the card, wadding side down, in the centre. Check the card is centred on the square. Carefully apply glue around the outer edge of the card, covering about ½in (1.25cm) from the edge, see **Fig 4** overleaf. Fold the fabric corners and press firmly. Fold the sides of the fabric square over and press firmly. Before the glue dries, sew the corner mitres together to make them nice and sharp.

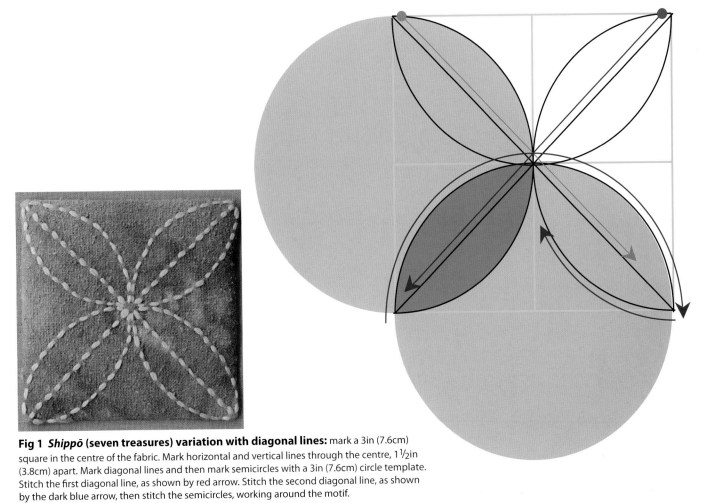

Fig 1 *Shippō* **(seven treasures) variation with diagonal lines:** mark a 3in (7.6cm) square in the centre of the fabric. Mark horizontal and vertical lines through the centre, 1½in (3.8cm) apart. Mark diagonal lines and then mark semicircles with a 3in (7.6cm) circle template. Stitch the first diagonal line, as shown by red arrow. Stitch the second diagonal line, as shown by the dark blue arrow, then stitch the semicircles, working around the motif.

Fig 2 *Hanabishizashi* **(flower diamond stitch):** mark a 3in (7.6cm) square and divide it into a 1½in (3.8cm) grid. Mark diagonal lines, crossing each grid square. Stitch the first row of each section along the diagonal line, shown in red on the shaded background, and build up the pattern on either side of this row, with the gaps between the stitches in each 'petal' about half the length of the stitch and a longer gap at the end of each petal. Stitch the diagonal rows leaning to the right first, then leaning to the left. Strand the thread across the back in the longer gaps between stitches (see page 27).

Fig 3 *Momiji* (maple leaf) motif (actual size): Transfer the design either using Chaco paper (see page 21) or make a cardboard template to draw around. If using a template, draw in the leaf veins freehand. Start stitching around the edge of the leaf, following the outline. Stitch the veins and stalk last, crossing the centre of the leaf and stranding between the leaf centre and the stalk.

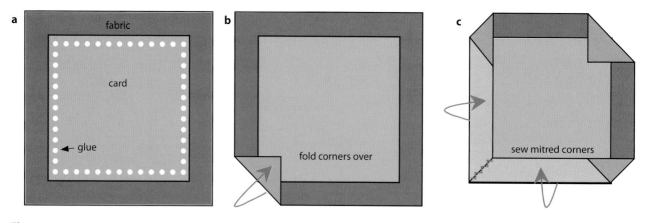

Fig 4 Gluing and folding a sampler square around card.

3 Gluing on the squares:

Arrange the squares using the picture here as a guide – an asymmetric arrangement looks best. Apply glue to the back of each square and stick to the book cover. Place a weight, such as a pile of other books, on top of the album to keep the squares flat as they dry, covering the squares with a plastic bag so no excess glue can stick to your books!

Tip
Think about the space around the squares when arranging your cover design. Use a leftover square for another project rather than overcrowd the layout.

Table Runner

Sashiko patterns used: two *shippō* (seven treasures) variations, *hanabishizashi* (flower diamond stitch), *komezashi* (rice stitch) variation and *sakura* (cherry blossom) motif
Finished size: 34¾in x 13¼in (87cm x 33.7cm)

Idea
Sashiko sample squares make a great swap project for your quilt group.

You will need

- **Five pieces of sashiko fabric, 4in (10.2cm) square**
- **Striped fabric:**
  two strips 35¼in x 5⅜in (89.5cm x 13.7cm)
  two strips 5½in x 4in (14cm x 10.2cm)
  four strips 2⁵⁄₁₆in x 4in (6.8cm x 10.2cm)
- **Backing fabric 35¼in x 13¾in (89.5cm x 35cm)**
- **Medium sashiko thread in light ochre and shaded pink**
- **Sewing thread to match fabrics**
- **Basic sewing and marking kit**

Tip
Cut wide stripes so that the most dominant colour will frame the centre of the runner. The dominant colour in my fabric is pink but the ochre stripe also stands out, so the smallest pieces were cut with the ochre stripe in the same place each time. Cut along the stripe with scissors for accurate lines.

1 Cutting the fabric:
Cut the 35¼in x 5⅜in (89.5cm x 13.7cm) striped fabric strips with the stripes parallel to the longer sides. Cut the smaller pieces with the stripes running parallel to the 4in (10.2cm) sides.

2 Marking and stitching:
The runner features five sample squares – two as described for the album (Fig 1 and Fig 2 on page 33) and three designs using

Fig 3, **Fig 4** and **Fig 5** shown overleaf. Take each 4in (10.2cm) fabric piece and, following the five diagrams, mark the patterns (see marking methods, page 21). Stitch the sashiko, following the detailed captions with each diagram. Press each finished square.

3 Assembling the patchwork:
Following **Fig 6**, machine sew the patchwork using ¼in (6mm) seams throughout. Assemble the centre strip with the sashiko and striped pieces first, noting that the two 5½in x 4in (14cm x 10.2cm) strips are on the ends. Pin and sew squares and strips right sides together in pairs, then sew pairs together to make the long central patchwork strip. Press seam allowances towards the striped fabrics. Pin one striped side panel to the edge of the patchwork strip, right sides together. Pin at the centre and ends of the long strip first, then pin along the length. Machine sew the seam. Sew on the other side strip the same way.

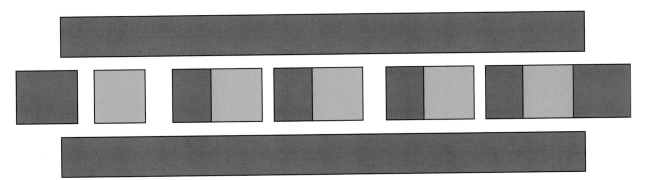

Fig 6 Assembling the patchwork pieces for the runner.

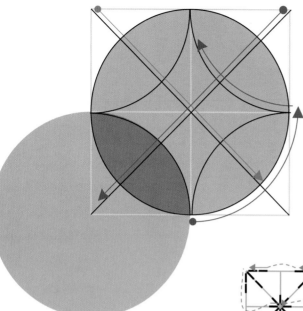

Fig 3 *Shippō* (seven treasures) variation with diagonal lines: mark a 3in (7.6cm) square in the centre of the fabric. Mark horizontal and vertical lines through the centre, 1½in (3.8cm) apart. Mark diagonal lines and mark semicircles with a 3in (7.6cm) circle template. Stitch diagonal lines first, as shown by red and dark blue straight arrows. Stitch the circles and arcs, working around the motif and alternating between the outer circle and inner arcs in a continuous line, as shown by blue curved arrows.

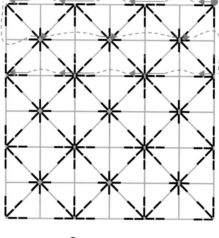

Fig 4 *Komezashi* (rice stitch) variation: mark a 3in (7.6cm) square in the centre of the fabric. Mark horizontal and vertical lines, ½in (1.3cm) apart, to make a grid. Mark diagonal lines, as shown. Starting at top right, stitch horizontal rows back and forth across the grid, following the red arrows. Make stitches as indicated by the short black lines, stranding loosely across the back between stitches, as shown by dashed lines. Leave a turning loop at the end of each row, then stitch the next row. Note that the first, third, fifth rows etc. have two stitches to form the 'flower' effect, while the alternate rows have only one. Stitch vertical rows the same way. Complete the design by stitching the horizontal lines – this time each row alternates between two-stitch and one-stitch 'flower petals'.

Fig 5 *Sakura* (cherry blossom) (actual size): transfer the design either using Chaco paper (see page 21) or make a cardboard template. If using a template, draw in the centre detail freehand. Start stitching around the edge of the flower, following the outline. Stitch the centre last, crossing the centre of the flower.

4 Making up the runner:

Place the front panel and backing fabric right sides together and pin all round. Machine sew with a ¼in (6mm) seam allowance, leaving an 8in (10cm) gap at the centre of the lower edge. Trim off corners within the seam allowance, but don't cut right up to the stitches – to about ⅛in (3mm).

Turn out through the gap and ease out corners so they are sharp. Lay the runner flat and smooth. Turn under raw edges at the bottom, pin or tack and slipstitch the gap closed. From the back, sew right round the runner ⅛in (3mm) from the edge with small hand stitches through backing and seam allowances only to keep the backing in place.

Tip
Always sew patchwork with striped fabrics on top, so you can follow the line of the stripe as you sew and the striped edge parallel to the seam doesn't look wobbly!

Sashiko Inspirations

Sashiko samplers

Old sashiko pieces suggest that stitchers have enjoyed combining patterns in sampler styles for a long time. Shown here is some of the stitching on a wonderful sampler jacket, from the collection of the Chido Museum, Tsuruoka City in Japan, which sets sampler squares among a stepped design. Some squares have more than one pattern, so its maker must have had difficulty fitting all her favourites into one jacket! Old sorihikihappi *(sled-hauling waistcoats) often combined two or three patterns. The five Yen coin, included for scale, is shown slightly smaller than life size.*

Other designs with patterns in squares

Overlapped or scattered squares or squarish rectangles are a popular motif for kimono, obi and other textiles. The fukusa *(a ceremonial gift cloth) shown here combines squares with textured effects, small patterns and larger motifs. The technique used is* yuzen, *a rice paste resist-dyeing method, where gold accents were applied later. The design would make an unusual sashiko sampler layout. The squarish rectangle is popular as a design motif, reflecting the proportions of* shikishi *(calligraphy panels).*

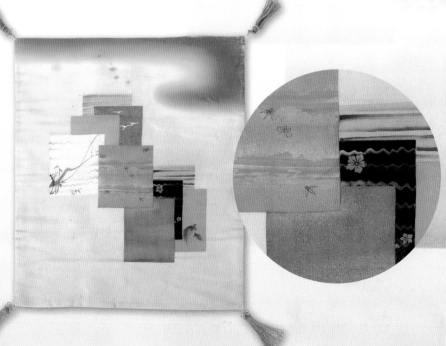

Koshi Throw

Woven checks and stripes provide an easy way to line up sashiko stitches in simple patterns and the stepped pattern on this throw couldn't be easier to make – no pattern marking required! The check or stripe size gives an easy unit to measure the sashiko pattern and you can use different sized checks. Designs like this were used for everyday clothing and household goods, where joining two fabric layers for extra warmth was more important than fancy stitches. If the thread matched the outer fabric, the sashiko was almost invisible when worn. This *kawari dan tsunagi* (linked steps variation) design from an old work jacket was too attractive to hide, so I used a fine cream thread to reveal the sashiko pattern on this versatile throw.

Koshi means check, and was a popular woven design for household textiles as well as clothing. By the mid 20th century, brighter colours were becoming more popular. Two complementary colourways of the same check produce a subtle effect.

Technique Taster

Try out this easy design with a small pillow (instructions overleaf). This one is stuffed with herbs mixed with chopped up fabric and wadding (batting) – scraps that were too tiny to use for anything else. The check measures about ⅝in (1.6cm).

The front check and stripe panel of this throw is simple strip patchwork in co-ordinating Indian cotton fabrics and a thick printed Japanese cotton is used for the back, so there's just two layers. See page 42 for throw instructions.

Herb Pillow

Sashiko patterns used: *kawari dan tsunagi* (linked steps variation)
Finished size: 9¼in x 10½in (23.5cm x 26.7cm)

You will need

- **Checked cotton fabric 19in x 11in (48.3cm x 27.9cm)**
- **Plain calico 19in x 11in (48.3cm x 27.9cm)**
- **Scraps of fabric and wadding (batting) to stuff pillow**
- **Fine sashiko thread in cream**
- **Sewing thread**
- **Basic sewing and marking kit**
- **Herbs (see Tip, right) and/or essential oils (aromatherapy oils)**

Idea
If you have a slightly smaller piece of checked cotton, just cut the calico to the same size and make a smaller pillow.

1 Stitching the sashiko:

Take the checked cotton fabric and fold it in half to measure 9½in x 11in (24.1cm x 27.9cm) to find the centre line.

If the checks are ⅝in (1.6cm) and the piece is centred on the pattern, the fold will be along the centre of a row of checks, not on the edge. Begin stitching along the edge of a row of checks, one and a half rows from the fold line. Three whole squares from the end of the line, turn the stitching through 90 degrees and stitch across three squares (see detail picture below), then turn again and stitch back along the next row. Continue until the first half of the panel is stitched, then complete the second half. Press each finished square.

If the checks are not ⅝in (1.6cm) you may wish to change the number of check squares from the end of each row and the number of squares in between rows. The smaller the spacing between stitch rows, the more stitching you will have to do overall.

Tip
Use your favourite herbs and oils sparingly! For a traditional Japanese scent, try blends with the following ingredients, all used for traditional incense – sandalwood, patchouli, frankincense, clove, cinnamon, star anise, safflower and cedarwood.

2 Making the pillow pad:

Fold the calico in half, right sides together, to measure 9½in x 11in (24.1cm x 27.9cm). Machine sew down each side and across the bottom edge with a ¼in (6mm) seam allowance, leaving a 4in (10.2cm) gap. Start and finish each seam with a few backstitches. Turn the pad right side out through the gap and make sure the corners are well turned out. Stuff with the fabric and wadding (batting) scraps, mixing in herbs and a few drops of essential oil. Slipstitch the gap closed, with small stitches so the filling can't escape.

3 Making the pillow cover:

Fold the sashiko panel in half, and machine sew with a ¼in (6mm) seam allowance, as for the pillow pad above, but leaving an 8in (20.3cm) gap unsewn across the bottom edge. Press and make sure the corners are well turned out. Ease the cover over the pillow pad. Pin and slipstitch the gap closed.

Tip
Don't throw away fabric offcuts like selveges, scraps too small to use and slivers of wadding – have a stuffing sack! Old Japanese futons and *zabuton* cushions were often filled with raggy offcuts and today commercial textile scraps are recycled into cushion padding. Snip long strips into short pieces before use and mix well.

Sashiko Inspirations

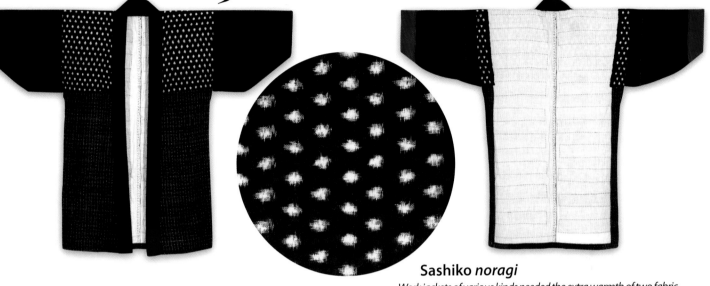

Sashiko *noragi*

Work jackets of various kinds needed the extra warmth of two fabric layers, stitched with sashiko rows. A simple woven pattern, whether a small kasuri (double ikat) motif or shima (stripe) and koshi (check) patterns, gave the sashiko stitcher something to follow, without the need to mark fabric or be able to see the weave easily. The noragi (field wear) jacket shown above is typical of many made in the second quarter of the 20th century, using assorted fabrics. Yukinko (snowball) kasuri on the shoulders (also shown in the circular detail) is combined with a check that included shaded threads, like the space-dyed threads used for kasuri. The lining (top right) includes soft cotton tenugui (towels). The sashiko stitches are in dark indigo thread, almost invisible from the outside.

Koshi rugs

Used under and over kotatsu (table heaters) and as kakebuton (futon coverlets), thick rugs had several layers of fabric with large, often quite crude, sashiko stitches holding them together. Large-scale checks were popular for household fabrics, including futon covers and zabuton (floor cushions). The checks are often offset rather than matched, giving a lively effect. The trio shown left includes two mid-20th century kotatsu rugs from Fukushima Prefecture (top and centre). One is very worn, with a plain centre rectangle added later on top of the checks. The second combines checks and nikko nikko kasuri (kasuri-style print) on alternate sides, edged with brown cotton binding. Both have the same simple grid sashiko, similar to the komezashi (rice stitch) variation used for the Kimono Wall Hanging on page 110. The third rug was probably used as a kakebuton and has very plain sashiko but large, colourful checks.

Sofa Throw

Sashiko pattern used: *kawari dan tsunagi* (linked steps variation)
Finished size: 68in x 51⅜in (172.7cm x 130.5cm)

You will need

- **Striped cotton 52⅛in x 10½in (132.4cm x 26.7cm)**
- **Striped cotton 52⅛in x 10¼in (132.4cm x 26cm)**
- **Checked cotton A: two outer strips 50¼in x 11¼in (127.6cm x 28.6cm)**

  one centre strip 50¼in x 10⅞in (127.6cm x 27.6cm)
- **Checked cotton B: two strips 50¼in x 10⅞in (127.6cm x 27.6cm)**
- **Backing fabric 69½in x 52⅛in (176.5cm x 132.4cm) – this may be pieced**
- **Fine cream sashiko thread 170 metre skein**
- **Sewing thread to match fabrics**
- **Basic sewing and marking kit**

Tip
The size of the checks and stripe I used are ⅜in (1cm), so it was easiest to cut them for a ⅜in (1cm) seam allowance. Cut along the checks and stripe with scissors for accurate lines.

1 Cutting out the fabric:

Cut along the nearest woven line in the check or stripe pattern each time. If your fabric has a different check size, you may wish to resize the pieces to suit your fabric better. For example, if it is a ½in (1.3cm) check, panel widths and lengths to the nearest ½in will work better. The checks look good lined up along the edges of each panel, giving the illusion that the same check weave is just changing colour and keeping the sashiko pattern aligned from one panel to the next. The width of the checks on my fabric varied slightly between the two colourways, so the centre and outer strips have fewer checks across the width (fabric A, blue colourway) than the two inner strips (fabric B, red colourway).

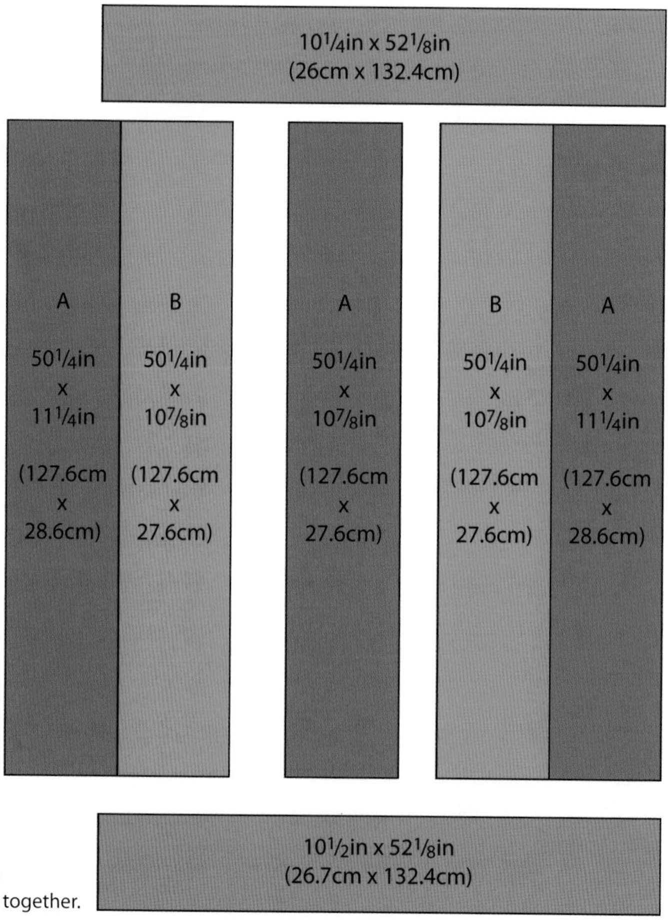

10¼in x 52⅛in (26cm x 132.4cm)				
A 50¼in x 11¼in (127.6cm x 28.6cm)	**B** 50¼in x 10⅞in (127.6cm x 27.6cm)	**A** 50¼in x 10⅞in (127.6cm x 27.6cm)	**B** 50¼in x 10⅞in (127.6cm x 27.6cm)	**A** 50¼in x 11¼in (127.6cm x 28.6cm)

10½in x 52⅛in (26.7cm x 132.4cm)

Fig 1 Piecing the patchwork panels together.

2 Sewing the patchwork:

With right sides together, pin the checked panels together in pairs, as shown in **Fig 1**, lining up the checks and machine sew with a ⅜in (1cm) seam allowance. Press seams to one side. Continue until the five strips are sewn together. Pin the striped panels on each end (see picture detail, right), lining up the stripe with the check and machine sew with a ⅜in (1cm) seam allowance. Press seams towards the striped fabric. Assemble the backing panel, piecing if necessary, and press any seams *open* to reduce bulk.

3 Tacking the layers:

Pin the patchwork top to the backing fabric, wrong sides together. Lay the backing panel right side down to do this and line up the top. Tack (baste) the two layers together (see page 22), tacking about ½in (1.3cm) from the seam lines and at intervals of about 3in (7.6cm) down and across the throw. Tack all around the throw, 1in (2.5cm) from the edge.

Idea

If you prefer, the throw can be bound like a patchwork quilt or an old sashiko rug, using binding strips cut on the straight grain.

To keep your sashiko pattern symmetrical, begin stitching from the middle of the centre strip and work along the strip.

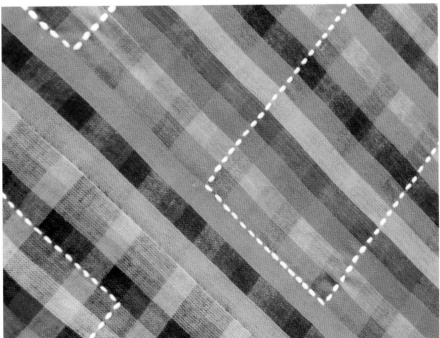

4 Hemming the throw:

Beginning with the patchwork top, turn under the edge ⅜in (1cm), i.e., the width of your stripe or check, and tack (baste) about ⅛in (3mm) from the folded edge: you are folding and sewing through the top only at this stage. When complete, turn the throw over and repeat the procedure with the backing fabric, turning the edge under to match the edge of the patchwork that you previously folded and tacked – use it as a guide but this time tack the backing fabric to the front of the quilt as you turn it. When the tacking is finished, slipstitch by hand all the way around the throw, stitching the backing to the top. Remove the tacking stitches. Stitch a single sashiko line all around the throw. Quilt in the ditch, i.e., sew the two layers together along each seam line with running stitch, using thread to tone with the fabrics rather than sashiko thread.

5 Stitching the sashiko:

Fold the throw in half to find the middle of the check strips and begin the sashiko stitching from the middle of the centre strip, working along the strip, as shown in the detail photo below. On my throw, this point ran through the centre of a line of check squares, rather than along the edge of a row of checks, so I decided to make the intervals between each step section seven check squares, an uneven number. Each section of the step pattern is then seven squares wide, approximately 2⅝in (6.7cm), and the stitch line turns through 90 degrees, three squares from the edge of each strip. Stitch the sashiko, using the method for starting and finishing without a knot (page 23). Because the throw has two layers, you can pull the thread between the top and bottom layer at the beginning and end of the stitching, so the end completely disappears between the layers. Stitch plain rows along the striped fabrics at the top and bottom, six stripes apart. Your throw is now complete.

Tip

Unless you want to be stitching the throw for a long time, resist having fewer rows of checks between the pattern 'steps' – a four-row spacing would almost double the amount of sashiko. If the checks are bigger, fewer check rows are fine.

Sakiori Bolster

I've called this cushion *sakiori* because the colourful, striped fabric reminds me of multicoloured Japanese rag weaving. Working sashiko on narrow-striped fabric offers the perfect grid for working *hitomezashi* (one-stitch) sashiko patterns. Vintage sashiko was sometimes stitched on striped cotton, using the stripes to line up the stitches. Any *hitomezashi* pattern would lend itself to decorating a long, narrow band and here the *hishizashi* (diamond sashiko) pattern has been chosen (see Sashiko Inspirations, page 49 for more on this pattern). The bolster cushion is an ideal project to explore this technique. It has two sashiko striped fabric panels, combined with two strips of unembroidered indigo fabric. Fabric stripes are about ⅛in (3mm) wide.

A key feature of this big bolster is that it has an intriguing twist – literally! – created by the way the fabric panels are joined during the making up process. Instead of sewing the cushion cover edges together, I've used traditional button-loop fastenings for a more decorative look.

Technique Taster

To practice the technique of working sashiko on narrow-striped fabric, try out *hishizashi* on these sewing accessories – a needle case for sashiko needles and a cute pincushion in a Japanese teacup. Both projects feature a blue-green background fabric for the white thread sashiko, while the pincushion has a frill of fabric with pinked edges giving an organic look. See overleaf for instructions.

This big, bold bolster is not only perfect as a comfortable cushion but could also be used as a footstool. The striped pattern is accentuated by the use of some red sashiko. See page 48 for instructions.

Needle Case

Sashiko pattern used: *hishizashi* variation **Finished size:** 4in x 5½in (10cm x 14cm) open

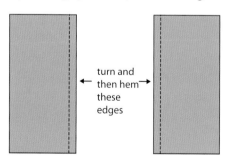

You will need

- Fabric with ⅛in (3mm) stripe 4½in x 6½in (11.4cm x 16.5cm)
- Two pieces of striped fabric 4½in x 2¾in (11.4cm x 7cm)
- Felt 3½in x 5in (8.9in x 12.7cm)
- Medium sashiko thread in cream
- Two lengths of fine cord, 10in (25.4cm) long
- Two pieces of thin card or plastic 3¾in x 2½in (9.5cm x 6.4cm)
- Sewing thread to match sashiko fabric
- Basic sewing and marking kit

1 Cutting the fabric:

Cut the striped fabric with the stripes parallel to the shortest side for the large piece and parallel to the longest side for the two smaller pieces. Overlock or zigzag the edges of the larger panel.

2 Marking the sashiko:

Take the 4½in x 6½in (11.4cm x 16.5cm) fabric piece and following **Fig 1**, beginning ¼in (6mm) from the edge, mark lines at right angles to the fabric stripe, ½in (1.3cm) apart (see marking methods, page 21).

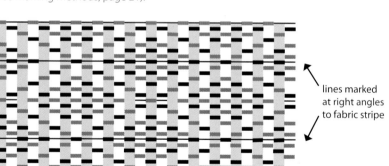

lines marked at right angles to fabric stripe

Fig 1 Using white thread throughout, start stitching the *hishizashi* variation with the red row shown in the centre of the diagram. Go on to stitch the second and third rows on either side of the first, building up the diamond shape. See also the picture detail above.

3 Stitching the sashiko:

With a doubled thread, stitch the sashiko, starting and finishing without a knot (see page 23). Follow the pattern shown in Fig 1. *Hishizashi* is one of numerous patterns that are stitched in straight lines, back and forth, as indicated by the red, grey and black lines in the stitch pattern. Press when finished.

Tip

Be careful to leave a turning loop at the end of each row (see *hitomezashi* stitching tips, page 27) as *hishizashi* is a very dense stitch and can tend to pucker up the fabric.

4 Making the needle case:

Hem one long side of each 4½in x 2¾in (11.4cm x 7cm) piece to make a flap by turning over a narrow hem allowance and top stitching by machine, as shown in **Fig 2**.

turn and then hem these edges

Fig 2 Hemming the two flaps of the needle case.

5

To attach the cords, lay the sashiko panel flat, right side up. Lay the two lengths of cord on the panel, as shown in **Fig 3** – note that the end of one cord is slightly above the dotted centre line and the other is slightly below. Tack (baste) the cord ends in place. Now place the two flaps on each end of the

sashiko panel, right sides together, as shown in **Fig 4** and machine sew, following the red dashed lines. Trim off the corners within the seam allowance but do not cut right up to the stitches – leave about 1/8in (3mm). Turn right side out and ease out corners so they are nice and sharp.

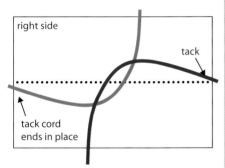

Fig 3 Positioning the cords on the panel.

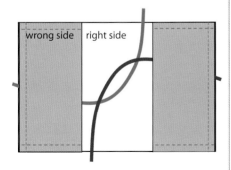

Fig 4 Sewing the flaps in position on the panel, right sides together, along red dashed lines.

6 Machine sew the piece of felt to the centre of the needle case. Push one piece of thin card or plastic into each pocket, to keep the needle case rigid. To fasten the case, wrap the cords around it and tie.

Pincushion

Sashiko pattern used: *hishizashi* variation
Finished size: 3in (7.6cm) diameter approx

You will need

- **One 8in (20.3cm) circle of 1/8in (3mm) striped fabric, cut with pinking shears**
- **Medium cream sashiko thread**
- **Wadding (batting) scraps**
- **Japanese teacup or small bowl 3 1/2in (8.9cm) diameter approx**
- **Sewing thread to match fabric**
- **Impact adhesive suitable for fabric and ceramic**
- **Basic sewing and marking kit**

Idea
There are a wide variety of Indian cotton stripes available in quilt shops and these are excellent for this technique. Choose the colours you like best.

1 **Marking the sashiko:**
Mark a 3 1/2in (8.9in) circle in the centre of the fabric. From the centre of the circle, mark lines at right angles to the fabric stripe, 1/2in (1.3cm) apart (see marking methods, page 21).

2 **Stitching the sashiko:**
With a doubled thread, stitch the sashiko, starting and finishing without a knot (see page 23). Follow the stitch pattern in **Fig 1** opposite, but this time stitch the sashiko within the 3 1/2in (8.9in) circle only. Press when finished.

3 **Making the pincushion:**
Draw a 6in (15.2cm) diameter circle centred on the embroidered pattern and hand sew a gathering thread along this line. Slightly gather up the fabric, stuff the centre with wadding offcuts and gather up and fasten off the thread. Arrange the pinked edges to form a frill around the pincushion. Following the manufacturer's instructions, glue the pincushion into the cup and allow to set.

Bolster Cushion

Sashiko pattern used: *hishizashi* variation **Finished size:** 9in x 9in x 15in (23cm x 23cm x 38cm)

You will need

- Two strips of striped fabric 29in x 6½in (73.7cm x 16.5cm)
- Dark indigo fabric:
  two strips 28½in x 6½ (72.4cm x 16.5cm)
  two strips 22½in x 2½in (57.2cm x 6.4cm)
  five strips 2¾in x 1in (7cm x 2.5cm) for button loops
- Fine cream sashiko thread, two 170m skeins
- Fine red sashiko thread
- Four strips of plain red fabric, 28½in x 6½in (72.4cm x 16.5cm) for cushion pad
- Polyester stuffing for cushion pad
- Five shirt buttons ½in (1.3cm) diameter
- Sewing thread to match sashiko fabric
- Basic sewing and marking kit

1 Cutting the fabric:

Cut the striped fabric with the stripes at right angles to the longer sides. Note: the striped fabric is cut slightly longer than the other pieces as the sashiko will pull in the fabric by about ½in (1.3cm) over the length of the strip. Overlock or zigzag the edges of the panels.

2 Marking the sashiko:

Following **Fig 1** on page 46 and beginning with a line down the centre, mark lines at right angles to the fabric stripe i.e., parallel to the long sides, ½in (13cm) apart (see marking methods, page 21).

3 Stitching the sashiko:

With a doubled thread, stitch the sashiko, starting and finishing without a knot (see page 23). Follow the stitch pattern shown in Fig 1, beginning with the centre line. *Hishizashi* is stitched in straight lines, back and forth, as indicated by the red, grey and black lines in the stitch pattern. Stitch all the red lines with red thread and use cream thread for the black and grey lines (see also the detail picture above). Press the sashiko when finished.

Idea

Sakiori often used coloured warp threads to make plaid patterns. Increasing the red stitch lines from one to three or five will produce a stronger checked effect.

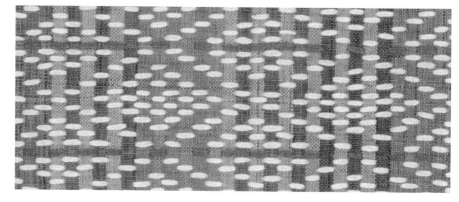

4 Making the bolster cover:

Overlock or zigzag the indigo fabric strips. Assemble the sashiko panels and the wider indigo fabric strips as shown in **Fig 2**. Machine sew two strips together at right angles, starting and finishing all seams ¼in (6mm) from the edge (to enable the seams at the centre of the bolster end to lie flat). Start and finish each seam with a few backstitches for added strength. Sew the four strips together. Press the seams to one side.

5

The edge of each panel needs to pivot to meet the edge of its neighbour, so clip the edge at the turn by ⅛in (3mm) and follow **Fig 3**, easing the strip around the corner of the neighbouring panel. Pin three long seams in place, matching the colour coded marks on the diagram. The ends of the strips can now be arranged for the other end of the bolster. Sew these ends seams first, as for step 2, before sewing the three long seams. The remaining gap forms the bolster cover opening.

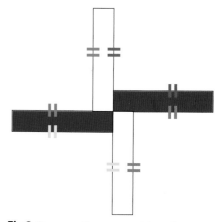

Fig 2 Forming the bolster cover by sewing the indigo fabric strips and the sashiko panels together at right angles to each other.

Fig 3 To sew up the cover, match up the seams with the same colour coded lines – red to red, green to green and so on.

6 Making the button loops:

Take one 2¾in x 1in (7cm x 2.5cm) strip, fold in half along the length and fold in the raw edges along the length, so the strip measures just ¼in (6mm) wide. Slipstitch the folded edges together along the strip to make one button loop. Fold the loop in half with the two ends parallel and tack (baste). Pin the loop to the centre of the edge of the sashiko strip, so the loop is facing away from the edge and the ends of the strip are hanging over the edge slightly. The loop will be sewn in place when the narrow indigo facing strip is sewn to the bolster cover. Make the other four loops, position them evenly along the edge and tack in place.

7

With the bolster cover right side out, pin one facing strip to each side of the opening, machine sew with a ¼in (6mm) seam and then press. Sew the opening closed for 1in (2.5cm) at each end. Hand sew along the edge of the facing strip to hold it in place. Sew on the buttons, matching their positions on the indigo strip with the button loops from the sashiko strip.

8 Making the bolster pad:

Using the four red fabric strips, make the bolster pad following steps 4 and 5 opposite. Sew the fourth seam along the side, leaving a 5in (12.7in) gap. Turn the bolster pad right

side out and press. Stuff solidly with polyester stuffing and slipstitch the gap closed. Ease the bolster cover over the pad and fasten the buttons to finish.

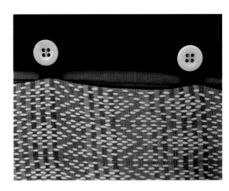

Sashiko Inspirations

Diamond patterns

There are many hitomezashi *designs based on the diamond or lozenge shape.* Hishi *is the water chestnut which has diamond-shaped leaves. The shape is a symbol of expansion and increase, so it was used to show a wish for prosperity. These patterns, including the* hishizashi *(diamond sashiko) pattern, were once used for reinforcement bands on farmers'* sorihikihappi *(sled-hauling waistcoats) made in Shōnai. From the late 19th century, the bands were fastened in place with large white shirt buttons, replacing the fabric ties or* kohaze *(tabi sock clips) formerly used. I've used these button features on the bolster cushion.*

Nanbu hishizashi (Nanbu diamond stitch) is a kind of kogin or counted sashiko which uses diamond motifs exclusively. The colourful effect (see picture below) echoes sakiori *ragwoven fabric, which was often combined with sashiko.*

Stitching on striped fabrics

Sashiko was sometimes stitched on stripes. Plain hand-woven cotton fabric with visible threads, used for early 19th century sashiko, would have been easy to count too. Bright stripes add a modern touch to Reiko Domon's bag below. Some sashiko from Shōnai looks like it was counted and diamond patterns on early 20th century head-scarves from Akita Prefecture certainly were. Counted hitomezashi *sashiko may be classed as* kogin, *a counted sashiko from Aomori Prefecture, which resembles pattern darning.*

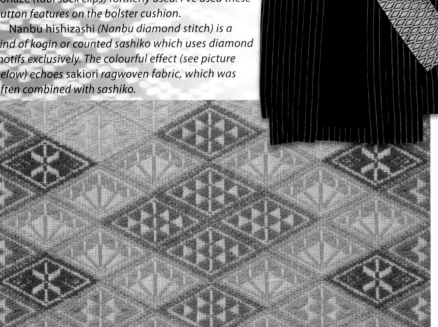

Irodori Cushions

Stitching different parts of a sashiko pattern with different coloured thread can really help when you are learning a pattern or adapting a new design, and looks beautiful too. These new patterns used on these cushions were adapted from vintage stencils used for dyeing *katazome* cloth. The brown cushion is a variation on the *asanoha* (hemp leaf pattern), with extra diamonds in the design. The rust cushion is stitched with *maru shippō* (circular seven treasures) but with segments of the pattern left out to create interesting negative shapes.

Irodori means 'colour scheme' and I chose thread and fabric colours carefully to emphasize different parts of the pattern. The dark blue thread used for the star details on the brown cushion is a similar tone to the background fabric, so this part of the pattern recedes, making the cream, ice blue and light green stitches more prominent. The shaded blues on the rust cushion were chosen to make the shapes in the circle centres stand out, while the persimmon thread motif in the centre blends in with the rust background.

Technique Taster

Single motifs from both patterns make scented sachets special, in shades of indigo on red *tsumugi* cotton (see overleaf for second sachet). Use up oddments of thread or try out colour schemes for your cushions. Great for gifts – try filling with lavender or cedar chips to scent clothes and linens (instructions overleaf).

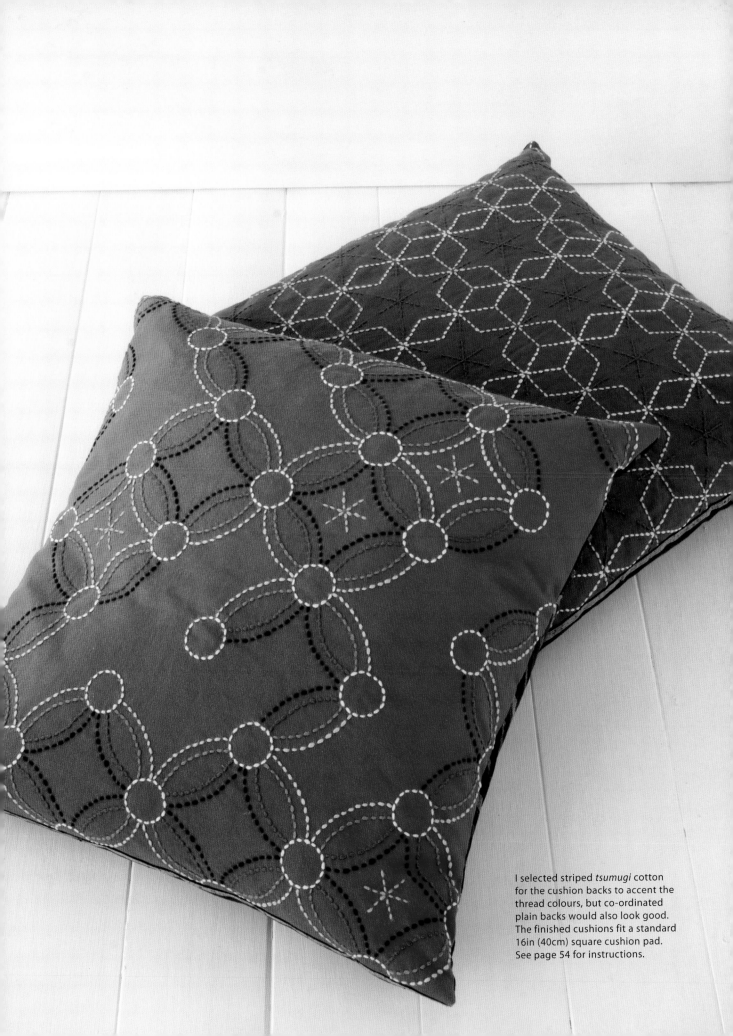

I selected striped *tsumugi* cotton for the cushion backs to accent the thread colours, but co-ordinated plain backs would also look good. The finished cushions fit a standard 16in (40cm) square cushion pad. See page 54 for instructions.

Scented Sachets

Sashiko patterns used: *asanoha* (hemp leaf) variation and *maru shippō* (circular seven treasures) variation
Finished size: 5in x 4½in (12.7cm x 11.4cm)

You will need
(to make two sachets)

- Four pieces of *tsumugi* cotton or similar, 5½in x 5in (14cm x 12.7cm)
- Medium sashiko thread in cream, ice blue, light blue, mid blue, dark blue and persimmon
- Sewing thread
- Basic sewing and marking kit
- Dried lavender or cedar chips for filling

Tip
The red *tsumugi* cotton is more tightly woven than some sashiko fabrics, so the lavender I used to fill the bags can't work its way out through the weave. Cotton chambray is similar.

Maru Shippō Variation Sachet

1 Marking the sashiko:
On one piece of fabric, draw two lines quartering the fabric, as shown by the light blue lines in **Fig 1**. Using 3½in (8.9cm) and 3in (7.6cm) diameter circles, mark the pattern, as shown. Mark the 3½in circle first, centred on the crossed lines, and then mark the smaller circle inside. Mark the circle segments using the same templates, overlapping the first circles. Use a 1in (2.5cm) circle template to draw the smaller circles.

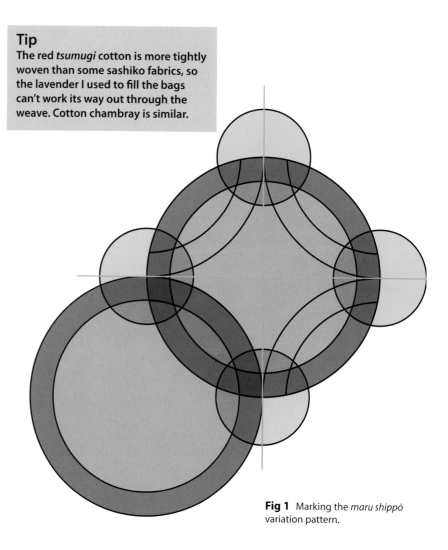

Fig 1 Marking the *maru shippō* variation pattern.

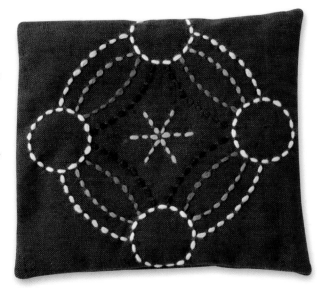

2 Stitching the sashiko:

With cream sashiko thread, stitch around the smaller circles first. Shading from ice blue to dark blue, stitch around the outside of the *shippō* motif first, and complete the design, working inwards, stranding across the back behind the smaller circles. Finally, mark three crossed lines in the centre and stitch with persimmon thread, stranding between the end of one line and the next. Leave out this final stage if you prefer. Press when stitching is complete.

Asanoha Variation Sachet

1 Marking the sashiko:

Draw a 4in (10.2cm) square, centred on the fabric, and mark a 1in (2.5cm) grid, as shown by the light blue lines in **Fig 2**. Mark the diagonal lines around the pattern, to make a hexagon, as shown by the black lines. Mark the diagonal lines to form the star within the hexagon, then mark the dashed black lines crossing the centre.

2 Stitching the sashiko:

With cream sashiko thread, stitch around the outer hexagon. With ice blue thread, stitch the inner star shape. With mid blue thread, stitch the lines crossing the centre of the star individually – stitch the first four stitches, leave a gap and stitch another four stitches to reach the centre. If your sashiko stitches are larger than mine, make three stitches instead of four. Press when finished.

3 Making the sachets:

With right sides together, machine sew around one sashiko panel and one plain piece of fabric with a ¼in (6mm) seam allowance, leaving a 3in (7.6cm) gap. Start and finish with a few backstitches. Trim off the corners within the seam allowance, but do not cut right up to the stitches – to about ⅛in (3mm) will be fine. Turn the sachet right side out through the gap. Ease the corners out so they are nice and sharp. Loosely fill the sachet with lavender or cedar chips. Turn under the raw edges, pin or tack (baste) and slipstitch gap closed.

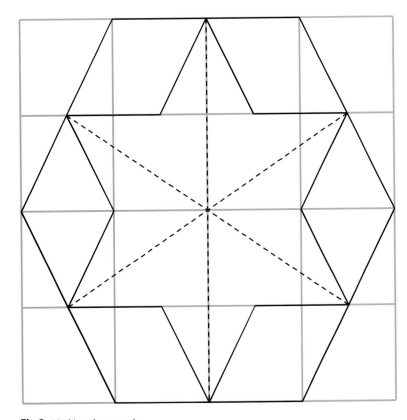

Fig 2 Marking the *asanoha* variation pattern.

Idea
If you add a loop of cord or ribbon you can hang the sachet in your closet or on a bedpost.

53

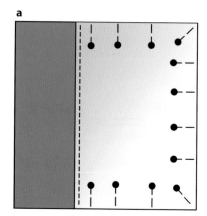

Irodori Cushions

Sashiko patterns used: *asanoha* (hemp leaf) variation for brown cushion and *maru shippō* (circular seven treasures) variation for rust cushion

Finished size: 16in (40.6cm) square

You will need

for the brown cushion
- Brown sashiko fabric 17in (43.2cm) square
- Medium sashiko thread in cream, ice blue, mid blue and light green

for the rust cushion
- Rust sashiko fabric 17in (43.2cm) square
- Medium sashiko thread in cream, ice blue, light blue, mid blue, dark blue and persimmon

for both cushions
- Two pieces of striped *tsumugi* cotton or similar 17in x 11in (43.2cm x 27.9cm)
- Sewing thread
- Basic sewing and marking kit
- 16in (40.6cm) square cushion pad

Tip
Choose a cotton stripe with similar colours to your sashiko threads for a co-ordinated look.

Making the Brown Cushion

1 Marking the sashiko:
Zigzag or overlock the edges of the fabric. Draw a 16in (40.6cm) square in the centre of the fabric (see marking methods, page 21). As in **Fig 1**, draw horizontal lines 1in (2.5cm) apart. Draw vertical lines 1in (2.5cm) apart but with 1/2in (1.3cm) between the first and last pair of lines. Mark the zigzag lines to make the diamonds, using the 1in grid as a guide.

2 Stitching the sashiko:
Following the red arrows in Fig 1, stitch the vertical zigzag lines first in cream thread (see picture above). Stitch the horizontal stepped lines next, in ice blue thread. Stitch the straight horizontal lines, in light green, stranding the thread across the back of your work, as shown by the dashed red lines.

3
Mark the second stage of the pattern, filling in the star shapes and following the red lines in **Fig 2**. Stitch these lines with mid blue thread, stitch the lines crossing the centre of each star – stitch the first four stitches, leave a gap, and stitch another four stitches to reach the centre. If your stitches are larger than mine, make three instead of four. Press when finished.

4 Assembling the cushion:
Hem one long edge of each 17in x 11in (43.2cm x 27.9cm) panel and zigzag or overlock the other edges. Add a button fastening to the overlap if you like – work buttonholes before sewing the backing panels in place and add the buttons when the cover is complete. Place the patchwork and one of the backing pieces right sides together and pin, as shown in **Fig 3a** below. Place the second backing piece right sides together, overlapping the first piece, and pin. Machine sew around the edge, with a 1/2in (1.3cm) seam allowance, as shown by the dashed line in **Fig 3b**. Clip the corners and turn right sides out. Insert the cushion pad through the gap to finish.

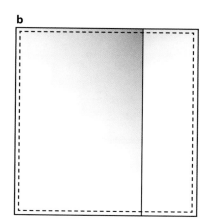

Fig 3a and b Making up the cushion.

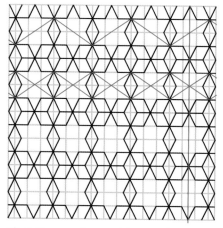

Fig 1 The first stage of the pattern to follow when marking the *asanoha* variation.

Fig 2 The second stage of the *asanoha* variation pattern.

Idea

These cushion panels can also be used for the centres of larger floor cushions. Surround the panel with a border to the size required.

Making the Rust Cushion

1 Marking the sashiko:

Zigzag or overlock the edges of the fabric. Draw a 16in (40.6cm) square in the centre of the fabric (see marking methods, page 21). As in **Fig 4**, draw horizontal and vertical lines 2in (5cm) apart. Using 4in (10.2cm) and 3½in (8.9cm) diameter circles, mark the pattern as shown. Mark the 4in circles first, centred on the crossed lines, then mark the smaller circle inside. Mark the circle segments using the same templates, overlapping the first circles. Use a 1in (2.5cm) diameter circle template to draw the smaller circles.

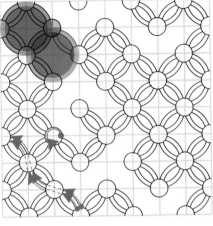

Fig 4 Pattern for the *maru shippō* variation.

2 Stitching the sashiko:

With cream sashiko thread, stitch around the smaller circles first (see picture above). Shading from ice blue to dark blue, follow the curved lines across the panel, stranding behind the cream circles. Finally, mark three crossed lines in the centre of some of the enclosed motifs and stitch with persimmon thread, stranding between the end of one line and the next. Leave out this final stage if you prefer. Press.

3 Assembling the cushion:

Make up the rust cushion in the same way as the brown cushion in step 4 opposite.

Sashiko Inspirations

Katazome stencils

Stencils used to apply the rice paste for katazome dyeing were made by specialist craftsmen and the tradition continues today. Sheets of shibugami, special stencil paper, are cut and lacquered before use. Fine gauze supports delicate parts of the design. The stencil is soaked before use, to cling to the fabric, so it has to be well made to withstand plenty of use. Once the rice paste has been pushed through the stencil and dried, the fabric is dyed. Fabrics used for yukata (cotton kimono) and komon (small pattern kimono) are dyed by katazome. Geometric and floral katazome designs can be a good source of sashiko patterns.

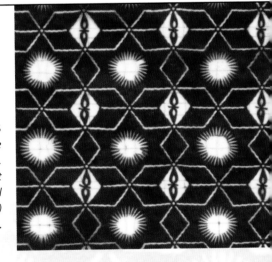

Shippō and *Asanoha* variations

Shippō is one of the ancient patterns known as yusōku, used by the Imperial Court from earliest times. It is an easy pattern to draw and many variations are possible. The Buddhist 'seven treasures' to which the name refers include gold, silver and precious stones, but it is also called wachigai (crossed circles). More shippō variations are used for the Mihon Table Runner (page 30) and Tansu Pocket Hanging (page 82).

Asanoha is another pattern with Buddhist origins, representing raditating light. It remains popular for children's kimono, reflecting the hope that the child will grow up strong like the hemp plant. Stretched, scattered and fragmented versions are just a few of the ways asanoha is used in sashiko. For more ways to use the basic asanoha pattern, see the Ranru Wall Hanging (page 96) and Sensu Tablemat (page 66).

Marumon Screen

Circular designs called *marumon* are considered unique to Japanese design and this impressive screen would give any room instant Japanese style. The imaginary flower design is called *hōsōge* and was introduced to Japan from China around 1,300 years ago. The overlapping circles feature *tsuru kame*, crane and turtle (sometimes translated as tortoise), which are auspicious symbols of longevity – the crane is said to live for 1,000 years, the turtle for 10,000. Details of both designs are emphasized with coloured sashiko thread.

The *hishi* (diamond) grid background links groups of plain diamonds with *raimon* (spiral) pattern infills, stitched in darker threads for a subtle contrast.

The screen panel is typical of *marumon* designs, where plants, animals and abstract shapes are attractively arranged to make the most of the circle format, frequently against a geometric backdrop, which emphasizes all the curves. The screen frame is easy to adapt from a picture frame – see the tip on page 61.

Technique Taster

A handy book cover bag is just the thing if you enjoy reading on your travels and it can be made to fit the book of your choice. The lucky motif trio of *shō chiku*, *bai* (pine, bamboo and plum) the 'three friends of winter', represents longevity, hardiness and vitality. Striped *tsumugi* cotton repeats the thread colours (instructions overleaf).

Japanese single-panel screens, called *tsuitate*, are used around the home to formally close off certain areas, such as a corridor, and are invaluable in an open-plan interior. The single panel also makes a perfect fire screen for an unused fireplace in a Western room. Instructions are on page 61.

Book Cover Bag

Sashiko patterns used: *shō chiku bai* (pine, bamboo and plum) *marumon* (circular motifs) and *raimon* (spiral) diamond variation
Finished size: 8in x 11in (20.3cm x 27.9cm) opened flat

You will need

- **Sashiko fabric 8½in x 11½in (21.6cm x 29.2cm)**

- **Striped *tsumugi* cotton or similar:**
  one strip 8½in x 5in (21.6cm x 12.7cm) for back pocket
  one strip 8½in x 3¾in (21.6cm x 9.5cm) for front pocket
  two strips 12½in x 2½in (31.8cm x 6.4cm) for handles

- **Plain cotton 8½in x 11½in (21.6cm x 29.2cm) for lining**

- **Medium sashiko thread in cream, green, light brown, persimmon and shaded pink**

- **Sewing thread**

- **Basic sewing and marking kit**

1 Assemble all your fabric pieces together, either using the measurements given in the list above or those you have calculated for your book size using **Figs 1a** and **1b**.

2 Marking the sashiko:

When you have all your fabric pieces together, zigzag or overlock the edges of all fabric pieces before you begin. Fold the sashiko fabric into quarters and finger press the folds near the outer edge. Open out the fabric. You will be able to see the pressed mark, halfway along the top and bottom edges of the panel and halfway down the sides. If your book cover bag is the same size as mine, this will measure 5¾in (14.6cm) to the centre at top and bottom and 4½in (11.4cm) to the centre side. Mark ¼in (6mm) in from the edge. Following **Fig 2**, join these midpoints with lines to form a large diamond. Now add diagonal lines from corner to corner on the panel, to divide the diamond into four.

Changing the cover size

This cover will fit a paperback 7¾in x 5in (19.7cm x 12.7cm) with a spine width of up to ½in (1.3cm). If your book is a different size, follow the instructions below to resize the fabric pieces. You will need to be able to sew a ¼in (6mm) seam accurately, so cut the pieces with a ⅜in (1cm) allowance and if the finished bag is slightly too large, you can re-sew the seams for a closer fit.

- Measure your book by making a sketch of Fig 1a and noting down the size of the cover and the thickness of the spine. To work out the total width of the sashiko panel, add the back width, spine width and front width together, plus another ¾in (1.9cm) for seams.

- The height of the book plus ¾in (1.9cm) will be the height of the panel.

- The strips for the pockets will need to be resized too – their height will be the same as the height of the sashiko panel – see Fig 1b.

- The back pocket strip will measure the total width of the back (no need to add an extra seam allowance, as the back pocket, once hemmed, will be narrower than the book back).

- The front pocket strip will measure about three-quarters of the front cover width.

- Handle lengths can remain the same for all books up to the same size as this sashiko book.

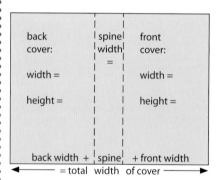

Fig 1a Calculating the size of the book cover.

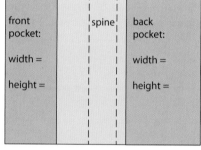

Fig 1b The cover as seen from inside – note the front pocket is narrower.

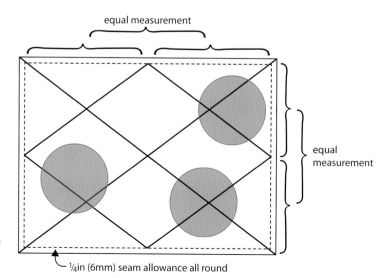

Fig 2 Marking the sashiko patterns.

3 Mark the circular motifs, using the full-size motifs in **Fig 3**. The circles are 3in (7.6cm) in diameter and the motifs may be marked either by with Chaco paper (see page 21) or with card templates.

Fig 3 The templates (actual size) for the plum, pine and bamboo motifs.

4 Now mark the diamond spirals, as shown in **Fig 4** below.

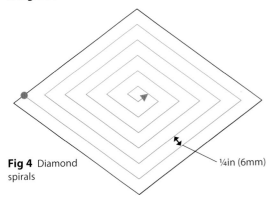

Fig 4 Diamond spirals

¼in (6mm)

5 Stitching the sashiko:

Following the illustrations, and the detail picture below, begin by stitching the circles in cream. Stitch the motifs inside the circles in green and shaded pink. Stitch the large diamond outline and the quarter lines. Stitch each diamond spiral individually, beginning outside and working in. Where circles cross over the spiral diamonds, strand across the back to the next spiral line rather than continuing the spiral with a very long strand. Press when finished.

Plum

Pine

Bamboo

6 Making handles and pockets:

Following **Fig 5**, fold and press the first handle strip in half lengthways. Fold the long edges inwards to the pressed line, press again, then fold the long edges into the middle and press. Machine sew along each long edge, about $1/16$in (2mm) from the edge. Zigzag the ends. Repeat with the other strip. Turn under $1/4$in (6mm) hem twice along one long side of each pocket piece and machine sew.

7 Lay the bag panel right side up and arrange the handles (shown in turquoise), as in **Fig 6a**. Pin the handles so the inside edge of each end is $1\frac{1}{2}$in (3.8cm) from the centre of the panel edge and overlap the ends of the panels by about $1/2$in (1.3cm). Tack the ends of the handles in place. Now place the pocket panels and bag panel right sides together, as in **Fig 6b**. Machine sew across the ends of the bag with a $1/4$in (6mm) seam. Now open out the bag and press seam allowances and straps towards pocket panels. Reinforce the handles by machine sewing a figure of eight through the pocket panels at each end, as shown by the cross in square symbol in **Fig 6c**.

8 Turn under $3/8$in (1cm) at each end of the lining fabric and hem. Fold back the bag panel as shown in **Fig 7** and pin. Put the lining panel right side down against the book cover, sandwiching the flaps between the lining and the sashiko panel, and pin. The lining should be slightly shorter than the length of the book cover, so there won't be too much fabric to bunch up on the inside. Machine sew along the red dashed lines with a $1/4$in (6mm) seam, starting and finishing with a few backstitches. Clip the corners. Herringbone stitch (by hand) the seam allowance at the ends so it is sewn down to the pocket panels – this stops the edge of the book catching on the seams.

9 Turn the book cover bag right side out, by first turning the 'tube' made by the lining right side out. The pockets will be inside out, so turn them out the right way, making sure the corners are turned out well. Carefully slide the book into the pockets, beginning with the back panel – take care if the book cover is very thin.

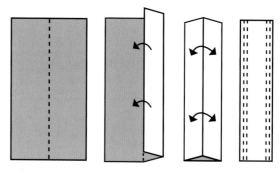

Fig 5 Making the bag handles.

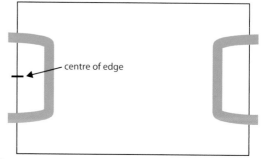

centre of edge

Fig 6a Positioning the handles.

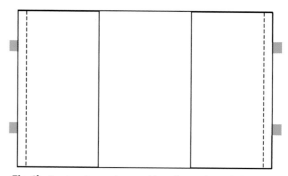

Fig 6b Sewing the pockets and handles to the sashiko panel.

Fig 6c Reinforcing the handles with figure of eight stitching.

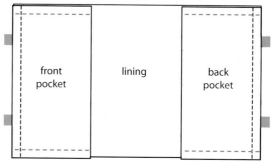

front pocket   lining   back pocket

Fig 7 The inside of the book cover bag, showing the lining and pockets sewn to the sashiko panel.

Screen

Sashiko pattern used: *hishi* (diamond), *raimon* (spiral) diamond variation and *marumon* pictorial designs
Finished size: 20in x 16in (50.8cm x 40.6cm)

You will need

- **Sashiko fabric 22in x 18in (55.9cm x 45.7cm)**

- **Medium sashiko thread, 40m skeins, in cream, persimmon, ice blue, light blue, medium blue, green, light brown**

- **Basic sewing and marking kit**

- **Fire screen or similar to fit 20in x 16in (50.8cm x 40.6cm)**

- **Strong thread to lace sashiko over frame panel**

Tip
I made the screen inexpensively from a picture frame. Select a frame with a square section on the outside, i.e. no curved or angled outside edges, and make two feet from strips of wood – they should be at least 5in (12.7cm) long for stability. Glue and screw them to the bottom edge of the frame.

1 Marking the sashiko:
Zigzag or overlock the fabric edges before you begin. Mark a 20in x 16in (50.8cm x 40.6cm) rectangle in the centre of the fabric. Divide this into a 2in x 4in grid (5cm x 10.2cm) and draw diagonal lines, as shown by the light blue and black lines in **Fig 1**. Following the instructions for marking with Chaco paper (page 21), trace and transfer the *marumon* motifs **Fig 2** and **Fig 3** on pages 63 and 64. Pink circles show their approximate position in Fig 1. Mark each of the coloured diamonds with a *raimon* spiral, as in **Fig 4** overleaf, drawing the lines parallel to the outer edges of the diamond, at ¼in (6mm) intervals.

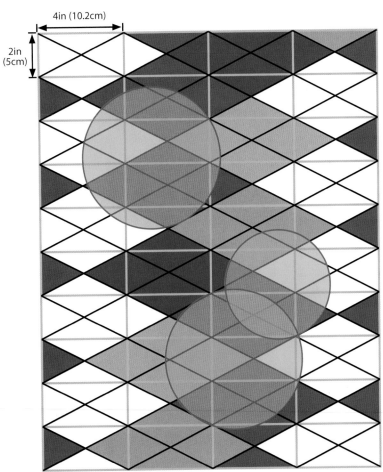

Fig 1 Marking out the sashiko grid. The pink circles show the positions of the *marumon* motifs. The diamond colour indicates which thread colour should be used.

2 Stitching the sashiko:
Begin stitching with the circles around the motifs, in cream (see detail picture overleaf). Stitch the *hōsōge* flower in cream, ice blue and persimmon, working your way around the motif. Stitch the turtle in cream and persimmon. The lines radiating from his shell represent long mossy trails, indicating his great age! Stitch along one strand and back along its neighbour. Stitch the crane in cream. Place two stitches side by side to indicate eyes.

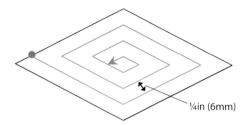

3 Stitch the *hishi* diamond grid in light blue. Stitch the individual *raimon* spirals in light blue, medium blue, green and dark brown, as indicated in Fig 1 and the detail picture below. Press when complete.

4 Framing the panel:

Refer to the instructions on page 27 for advice on framing your work.

¼in (6mm)

Fig 4 Pattern for marking the diamond spiral.

Idea

Threads used for the background are darker than those used for the motifs, so they blend with the fabric and the motifs stand out. I left a band of diamonds plain down each side, but if you wish to stitch these, use a dark blue thread.

Fig 2 Floral arabesque *hōsōge* template (actual size):
the green parts of the pattern are not used for the screen
project but are used for the Kasuri Throw on page 77.

Tip
The three-petalled clusters inside the
outer arabesques (shown in green on
the template here) looked too heavy
stitched in medium sashiko thread, so
I omitted them for the screen project.
The full motif is stitched in fine thread
on the Kasuri Throw on page 77.

Fig 3 Crane and tortoise marumon template (actual size).

Sashiko Inspirations

Women's formal *obi*

During the 18th century, when extravagant kimono designs were prohibited by various laws, the obi sash used to fasten kimono widened considerably and became the decorative focus. The introduction of the Jacquard loom from Europe in the late 19th century produced further innovation, enabling weavers to create complex brocade patterns that were no longer exclusively for the ultra rich. Maru (round) obi, worn formally, were heavy, with brocade patterns on both sides. Later, the fukuro (fold) obi, with only one side patterned, ousted the maru for formal wear. Large, elaborate designs remained popular, often with motifs set against another, smaller geometric pattern. The obi shown right is full of celebratory motifs, including cranes, imaginary hōsōge flowers, peonies and chrysanthemums, with maple leaves, plum blossoms and sayagata (saya brocade pattern) in the background. The crane and hōsōge marumon were adapted for my screen motifs.

Katazome indigo textiles

Marumon are striking motifs for home furnishings, as shown by this piece of katazome (stencil dye) from a futon cover. A rice paste resist was applied through a stencil and once dry, the fabric was immersed in an indigo dye vat, the indigo's reaction with oxygen in the atmosphere subsequently turning the cloth vibrant blue. Cotton katazome items were the mainstay of many brides' trousseaux, which is why motifs associated with good fortune and long life were so popular. The turtle (or tortoise) on this panel is ingeniously designed (see circular detail), with the mosses trailing from his shell forming a decorative fringe. He is paired with a crane, in the traditional combination known as tsuru kame, and, along with pine boughs, the pattern expresses a wish for long life.

Sensu Tablemat

Geometric sashiko patterns are based on grid structures, which means that patterns can be distorted by stretching, slanting or tapering the grid. This adds interest and variety, and sometimes offers a more harmonious solution to fitting a pattern to a certain outline. Some distorted versions of traditional patterns appear frequently in Japanese designs. *Asanoha* (hemp leaf) is one that is often lengthened and has been used here as the basis for an unusual fan-shaped placemat. The folding fan is an auspicious image in Japan, as the opening fan suggests increase, while *sensu*, paper and lacquer folding fans, are an essential accessory for tea ceremonies.

The ideal setting for oriental cuisine, you can see how the sashiko on this placemat has been distorted so it looks like an opening fan. The *asanoha* pattern was drawn on a base grid fanning out into a curve, so the size of the 'leaves' increase towards the edge of the fan. The little plaited tassel, a corner feature borrowed from old *furoshiki* (wrapping cloths), adds a nice finishing touch.

Technique Taster

This napkin is the perfect project to practice a distorting technique. It uses the first stages of the *asanoha* pattern on a different grid, stretching the pattern lengthways. See pages 19 and 20 for other patterns ideal for distorting. See overleaf for napkin instructions.

This attractive tablemat is sure to be a talking point at the dinner table. The vibrant red, black and yellow colour scheme was inspired by lacquered tableware and a vintage silk kimono. See pages 69 for instructions.

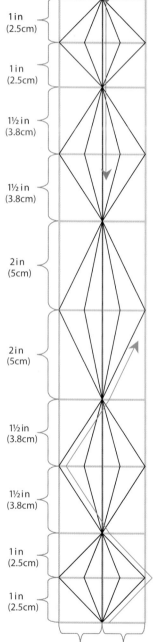

1in (2.5cm)
1in (2.5cm)
1½in (3.8cm)
1½in (3.8cm)
2in (5cm)
2in (5cm)
1½in (3.8cm)
1½in (3.8cm)
1in (2.5cm)
1in (2.5cm)

1in (2.5cm) 1in (2.5cm)

Napkin

Sashiko pattern used: simplified *asanoha* variation
Finished size: 18½in (47cm) square

You will need
- Sashiko fabric 20in (50.8cm) square
- Fine gold sashiko thread
- Sewing thread to match fabric
- Basic sewing and marking kit

Tip
You can easily customize ready-made napkins with sashiko. Heavier Indian cotton napkins are available in many colours and are an ideal fabric. Cut the tablemat from an extra napkin for a co-ordinated table setting.

1 Making the napkin:
Fold and press a ¼in (6mm) double hem all round the fabric. Hem stitch the edge by hand or machine.

2 Marking the sashiko:
Following **Fig 1**, mark the sashiko pattern (see marking methods, page 21). Begin by drawing the grid and then draw the diagonal lines.

3 Stitching the sashiko:
With a doubled thread, stitch the sashiko, starting and finishing without a knot (see page 23 and sewing sashiko, page 25). Begin with the central straight line (red arrow) and continue with the zigzag lines (green arrow). Press the napkin when finished.

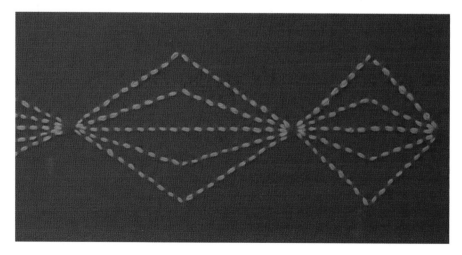

Fig 1 Sashiko pattern to be marked on the fabric. The red and green arrows indicate the direction of stitching – see step 3.

Fan Tablemat

Sashiko pattern used: distorted *asanoha*
Finished size: 7³⁄4in x 13¹⁄4in (19.7cm x 33.7cm)

You will need

- Red sashiko fabric 7in x 14in (17.8cm x 35.6cm)
- Black sashiko fabric 4in x 6¹⁄2in (10.2cm x 16.5cm)
- Red fabric for backing 8¹⁄2in x 14in (21.6cm x 35.6cm)
- Two pieces of muslin 8¹⁄2in x 14in (21.6cm x 35.6cm) (optional)
- Fine gold sashiko thread
- Sewing thread to match fabric
- Tracing paper for template and Chaco paper to transfer design
- Basic sewing and marking kit

Idea

If you prefer, you could stitch the sashiko on a single piece of fabric, rather than piecing the black and red fabrics together.

1 Marking the sashiko:

Trace the sashiko pattern from **Fig 1** overleaf. Only half the pattern is shown, so fold the tracing paper along the centre line, draw the pattern once, then flip the tracing and draw the pattern again. Using the Chaco paper, transfer the top part of the pattern, including the fan outline, to the red fabric, centring the pattern on the fabric (see marking fabric using Chaco paper, page 21). Add an extra ¼in (6mm) all round for the seam allowance and cut out on this line. Transfer the lower part of the pattern (the shaded section) to the black fabric the same way, adding ¼in (6mm) all round, and cut out.

2 Trace the backing fabric pattern from **Fig 2** on page 71 and cut one on the fold.

3 With right sides together, pin the red fabric to the black, matching curves, pinning the ends first with pins at right angles to the edge. Ease the rest of the curved edge together and insert more pins. Machine sew together, easing the curve as you go. To thicken the mat, tack (baste) pieces of muslin to the back of the fabric panel (optional).

4 Stitching the sashiko:

With a doubled thread, stitch the sashiko as in **Fig 3** on page 72. A detail of the stitching is shown below. Note on the picture above that the fan 'sticks' are sewn with a double line of sashiko for emphasis. Press the completed sashiko. The tassel is added when the placemat is complete. (Continue on page 72.)

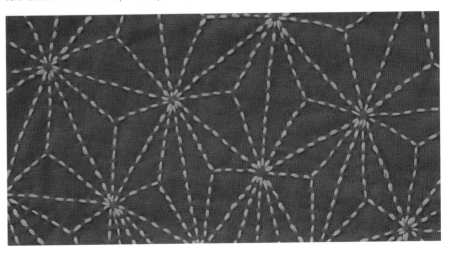

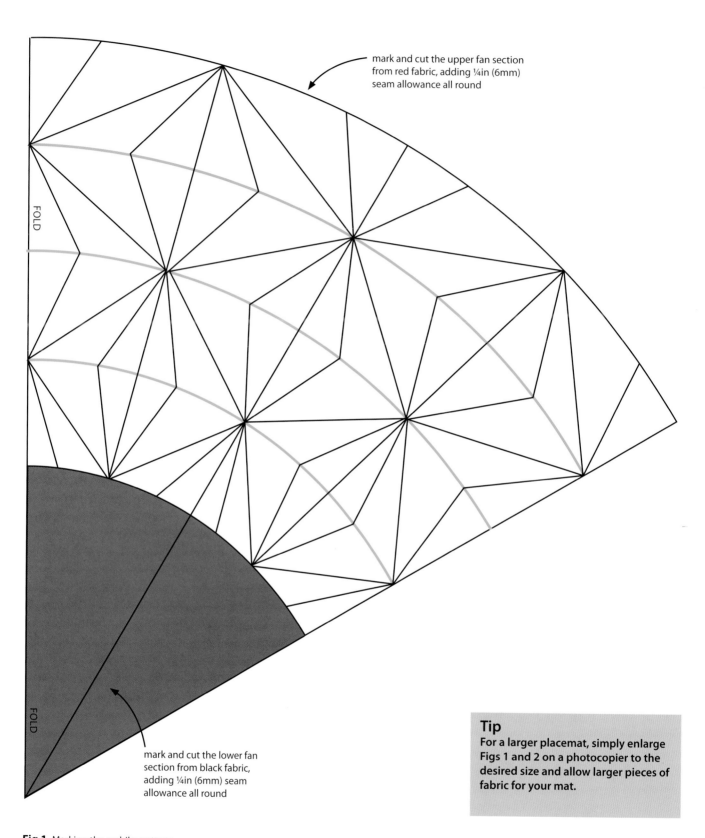

mark and cut the upper fan section
from red fabric, adding ¼in (6mm)
seam allowance all round

FOLD

FOLD

mark and cut the lower fan
section from black fabric,
adding ¼in (6mm) seam
allowance all round

Tip
For a larger placemat, simply enlarge
Figs 1 and 2 on a photocopier to the
desired size and allow larger pieces of
fabric for your mat.

Fig 1 Marking the sashiko pattern.

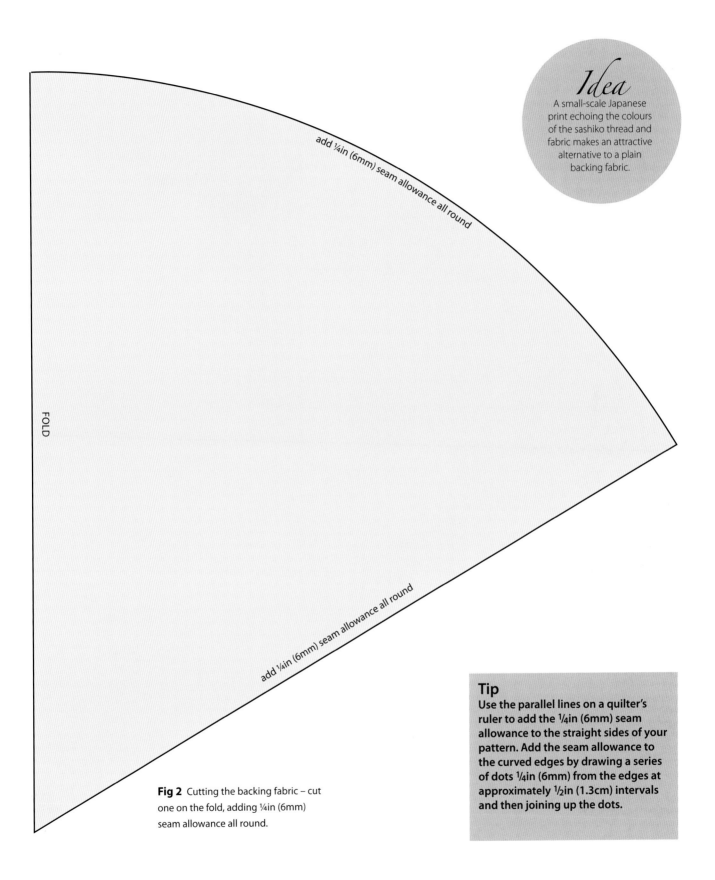

add ¼in (6mm) seam allowance all round

FOLD

add ¼in (6mm) seam allowance all round

Idea
A small-scale Japanese print echoing the colours of the sashiko thread and fabric makes an attractive alternative to a plain backing fabric.

Fig 2 Cutting the backing fabric – cut one on the fold, adding ¼in (6mm) seam allowance all round.

Tip
Use the parallel lines on a quilter's ruler to add the ¼in (6mm) seam allowance to the straight sides of your pattern. Add the seam allowance to the curved edges by drawing a series of dots ¼in (6mm) from the edges at approximately ½in (1.3cm) intervals and then joining up the dots.

71

Tip
In some sashiko patterns, thread needs to be 'stranded' across the back of the work if a gap is required on the front of the work – see page 26.

5 Making up the tablemat:

Place the sashiko panel and backing fabric right sides together and pin all round. Machine sew with a ¼in (6mm) seam allowance, leaving a 4in (10.2cm) gap on one straight edge. Trim off the corners within the seam allowance but do not cut right up to the stitches – leave about ⅛in (3mm). Trim back the optional muslin layers to the stitching, to reduce bulk. Bag out the mat, i.e., turn it the right way out through the unsewn gap. Ease out the corners so they are nice and sharp. Lay the mat flat and smooth it out. Turn in the raw edges at the gap and slipstitch the gap closed. From the back and using matching sewing thread, hand sew right around the panel ⅛in (3mm) from the edge, with small, neat stitches, through backing and seam allowances only, to keep the backing in place.

6 Making the tassel:

Stitch extra strands of thread through the bottom of the fan – two strands of thread leading from the end of each fan 'stick' is enough for a fine plait (see detail picture above). Leave the threads long enough to plait easily – about 4in (10.2cm) long. Make the plait with two groups of three strands of thread and one group of four. When the plait is about 1¼in (3.2cm) long, knot the end and trim off the excess thread. Press the placemat to finish.

Tip
A finishing touch, such as the plait on the placemat or the pretty little flower trims on the drawstring bag on page 74, can make a great difference to the finished project.

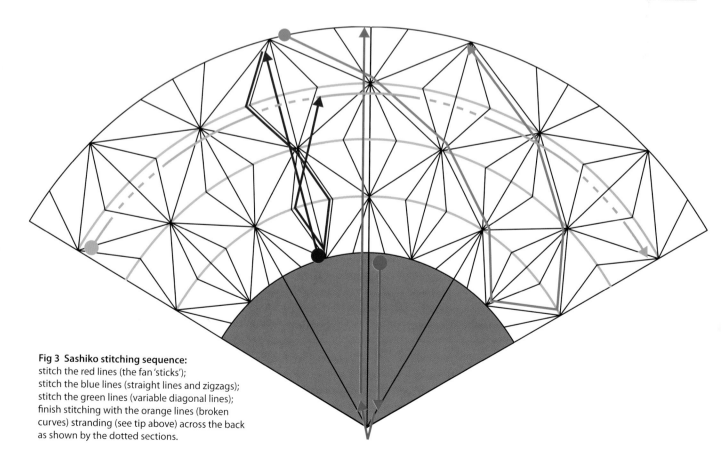

Fig 3 Sashiko stitching sequence:
stitch the red lines (the fan 'sticks');
stitch the blue lines (straight lines and zigzags);
stitch the green lines (variable diagonal lines);
finish stitching with the orange lines (broken curves) stranding (see tip above) across the back as shown by the dotted sections.

Sashiko Inspirations

The *sensu* (folding fan)

Invented in Japan, early fans were made from thin strips of cypress held together by cord, but paper fans were in use by the 10th century. In its many forms, the folding fan is the ubiquitous image of Japan. Small sensu, paper and lacquer folding fans, are an essential accessory for tea ceremony and are also worn tucked into the obi (sash) worn with kuro tomesode*, women's formal crested black kimono with gorgeous colourful patterns on the lower skirt. A larger but equally richly decorated paper fan may be displayed in the* tokonoma *alcove in a formal Japanese room.*

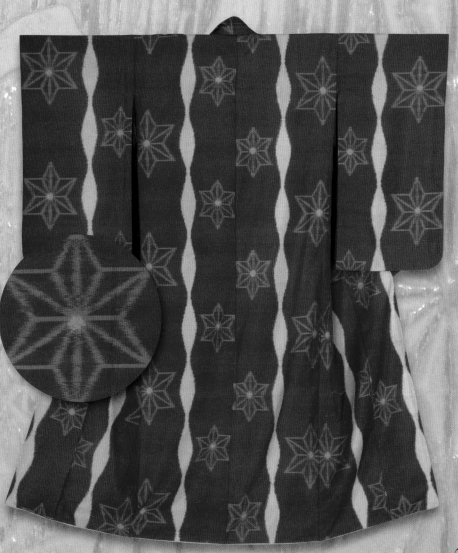

The *asanoha* pattern

This hemp leaf pattern, above and right, is associated with Buddhism, representing radiating light and the light within the soul. The detail shown above is from a pillar at the Buddhist temple on Mount Haguro, Yamagata Prefecture. The pattern originally came from China. It is particularly associated with children and was used to decorate children's clothes and bedding, in the hope that the child would grow strong like hemp. Asanoha is used to decorate everything from kimono to pottery and paper and is one of the most popular sashiko patterns today.

Kasuri Throw

Recreate the look of vintage *kasuri* (ikat) fabrics with this throw, combining patchwork with pictorial sashiko. *E-gasuri* (picture *kasuri*) usually have just one or two celebratory motifs alternating with an abstract design, but I have used the format for a sashiko picture sampler, with easy to make patchwork blocks, *igeta* (well curb). Finishing is quick, as rather than quilting the throw, I decided to tie it, in the style of old futon and *yogi* (kimono-shaped quilts), and it is 'bagged out' (that is, turned out to the right side) instead of being bound.

Different regions have different *kasuri* styles although picture motifs are similar. My favourites for sashiko designs are *koi*, *shiro* (castle), *kotobuki* (good fortune), *noshi* bundle, *hōsōge* floral circle, *matsu* (pine tree) and the *kiri kamon* (paulownia family crest). Sashiko and *kasuri*, where indigo and white colour schemes predominate, share the same aesthetic – a comfortable pairing.

Technique Taster

An individual motif looks striking on a *kinchaku* drawstring bag (instructions overleaf). I used the pine tree design on page 79 and stitched it on the same plain *tsumugi* cotton as the throw. The back is striped *tsumugi* and the lining is a patchwork print. The blue drawstrings are finished with flower trims. Each drawstring runs through both channels, making two loops, so it's easy to open and close the bag.

In this throw, the colour depth of the indigo blue *tsumugi* cotton, woven with blue threads on a black warp, makes a striking contrast with the cream calico patchwork. Blocks could be repeated for a larger quilt. See page 77 for instructions.

Drawstring Bag

Sashiko patterns used: *Matsu* (pine tree) motif
Finished size: 10in x 8in (25.4cm x 20.3cm)

Idea
A different motif could be stitched on the back of the bag. Any of the throw motifs can be used, or you can adapt other motifs. Position designs so they don't get lost in the gathers when the bag is closed.

You will need
- *Tsumugi* cotton fabric: one strip 10½in x 8½in (26.7cm x 21.6cm)
  two squares 3½in (8.9cm)
- Striped *tsumugi* cotton or similar 10½in x 8½in (26.7cm x 21.6cm)
- Two pieces of patchwork cotton 10½in x 8½in (26.7cm x 21.6cm)
- Two cotton squares 3½in (8.9cm) for flower trims
- Medium sashiko thread in cream
- Two 24in (61cm) lengths of cord for drawstring
- Sewing thread
- Basic sewing and marking kit

1 Marking and stitching:
Trace or photocopy the pattern from Fig 2 on page 79 – use the template at the size given. (Note: you could use any of the other designs on pages 79–81 for the bag.) Using either the Chaco paper method on page 21 or a lightbox, trace the pattern on to the plain *tsumugi* fabric. Place the motif centrally, about 1¾in (4.4cm) from the bottom edge. Stitch the sashiko, following the pattern outlines and referring to the illustration, and then press.

2 Assembling the bag:
Use a 2in (5cm) circle template to draw curves in the bottom corners of each piece of fabric, including the lining, and trim to the curve. Zigzag or overlock all pieces, down each side and across the bottom. With right sides together, sew the outer bag pieces along the dashed line from A to B, as in **Fig 1**. A and B are 2in (5cm) from the top edge, as shown by the red arrow. Repeat for the bag lining, but leave an unsewn gap on one side, about 4in (10.2cm). Press seam allowances open.

3
Turn the bag right side out and press. Place the bag inside the lining bag, right sides together, and sew each side of the bag to the lining along the dashed line from C to D, as in **Fig 2**. The gap between the side seams and points C and D is ¾in (1.9cm), left unsewn for the drawstring channel. Clip the top corners within the seam allowance but don't cut right up to the stitches – leave about ⅛in (3mm). Turn the bag right side out through the gap in the lining. Ensure corners are fully turned out and slipstitch the gap closed.

Now make a channel for the drawstring by topstitching in a straight line from A to B and from C to D on each side. Insert each drawstring, knot the ends and slipstitch the lining gap closed.

4 Making flower trims:
Fold a 3½in (8.9cm) square of cotton in half, right sides together, and sew a ¼in (6mm) seam to make a tube. Press the seam open. Turn half the tube right side out, so the fabric is doubled and the seam allowance hidden. With doubled sewing thread, make small running stitches around the raw end of the tube. Slip the tube over the knotted end of the drawstring (raw ends towards the knot) and gather up tightly (**Fig 3**). Take a few stitches through the cord and knot to finish off. Fold the tube down over the knot so it is hidden inside.

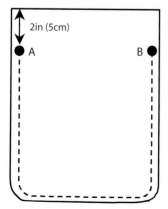

Fig 1 Sewing the bag pieces together.

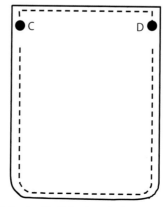

Fig 2 Sewing the lining into the bag.

Fig 3 Making a flower decoration for the ends of each drawstring.

Kasuri Throw

Sashiko patterns used: *koi*, *shiro* (castle), *kotobuki* (good fortune), *noshi* bundle, *hōsōge* floral circle, *matsu* (pine tree), *kiri kamon* (paulownia family crest), koi carp and circular arabesque

Finished size of throw: 59in x 43in (150cm x 109cm)

You will need

- **Plain blue *tsumugi* or thicker cotton patchwork fabric:**

  seven squares 12½in (31.8cm)

  seventy-two squares 2in (5cm)

  four strips 12½in x 2¾in (31.8cm x 7cm)

  sixteen strips 8in x 2¾in (20.3cm x 7cm)

- **Unbleached calico:**

  forty-eight squares 2in (5cm)

  sixteen strips 8in x 2in (20.3cm x 5cm)

- **Striped *tsumugi* cotton:**

  two strips 51½in x 4½in (130.8cm x 11.4cm)

  two strips 44½in x 4½in (113cm x 11.4cm)

- **Backing fabric 59½in x 44½in (151.1cm x 113cm)**

- **Wadding (batting) 59½in x 44½in (151.1cm x 113cm)**

- **Fine cream sashiko thread 170 metre skein**

- **Fine sashiko thread in medium blue, for tying the layers**

- **Sewing thread**

- **Basic sewing and marking kit**

Tip
Select a wadding suitable for tying at about 5in (12.7cm) intervals. Many waddings must be quilted as little as 3in (7.6cm) apart or they break down when washed. Ask your local quilt shop or mail-order supplier for advice.

1 Marking and stitching:

Enlarge **Figs 1–6** (pages 79–81) by 135% on a photocopier. Use the floral arabesque (**Fig 2** on page 63) *without* enlargement. Mark one design on each 12½in (31.8cm) square using either Chaco paper (see page 21) or a lightbox. Zigzag or overlock fabric edges before you begin. Stitch the sashiko, working around the motifs and then press.

2 Sewing the patchwork:

Using the 2in (5cm) calico and plain blue squares and 2in x 8in (5cm x 20.3cm) calico strips, sew the patchwork blocks, using **Fig 7** below as a guide. Use ¼in (6mm) seams throughout and press seam allowances towards the dark fabric each time. Machine sew the squares together in pairs, press and then sew the block together into strips.

3 Assembling the patchwork:

Lay out the pieces as in **Fig 8**. Arrange the sashiko blocks in a different order if you wish. Machine sew one blue 8in x 2¾in (20.3cm x 7cm) strip to each end of each patchwork block. Press towards the strip. Assemble the patchwork in three columns, sewing one 12½in x 2¾in (31.8cm x 7cm) strip to the top and bottom of each outer strip. Press seams towards the darker fabric each time. Pin and sew the strips together, pinning the ends and the centre first. Machine sew the strips together to make the central panel. Now machine sew the border strips, sewing the side panels first, then adding the top and bottom border, pressing towards the border each time. Attach the border strips with the borders on top as you sew, lining up your stitches with the woven strip to keep the seam straight.

2in (5cm) square

strip 2in x 8in (5cm x 20.3cm)

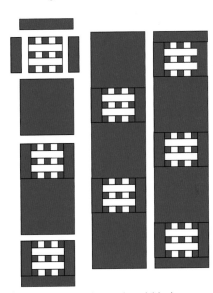

Fig 7 Sewing the patchwork squares and strips together for the *igeta* (well curb) blocks.

Fig 8 Assembling the patchwork blocks to create the panel.

Kasuri Throw

4 Making up the throw:

Lay the wadding (batting) flat and smooth it out. Lay the backing panel right side up on the wadding and tack the two layers together, at about 4in (10.2cm) intervals, horizontally and vertically. Place the patchwork panel right sides together with the backing panel and pin all round. Machine sew wadding, backing and panel together around the edges with a ¼in (6mm) seam allowance, leaving an 8in (20.3cm) gap at the centre of the lower edge. Trim off the corners within the seam allowance, but do not cut right up to the stitches – to about ⅛in (3mm) is fine. Turn the throw over so the wadding is on top and carefully trim away excess wadding within the seam allowance. Turn the throw right way out through the unsewn gap, easing out corners. Turn under the raw edges at the bottom and slipstitch the gap closed.

5 Tying the throw:

Tie the throw at all the red dot points in Fig 9. The dots along the top and bottom borders form a horizontal row, and the other dots are set out in vertical rows. Tie the throw following these rows. Lay the throw flat, sashiko side up and pin through all the layers at each dot. Use a long length of blue sashiko thread, doubled if you prefer. Leaving a 3in (7.6cm) tail of thread, take a backstitch over the first pin, going through all the layers, and tie the tail and the main thread securely with a square or reef knot. Cut the ends to 1in–2in (2.5cm–5cm) long and move on to the next knot. All ends should be about the same length.

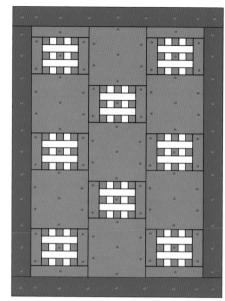

Fig 9 Red dots indicate the tying points spaced over the throw. Go from one tie to the next without cutting the thread until the end.

Sashiko Inspirations

E-gasuri

The threads for weaving e-gasuri (picture kasuri) are dyed before the fabric is woven. Blurry outlines are a kasuri characteristic and auspicious patterns predominated. These cotton fabrics were made for home decor. Kurume, Kyushu, and Iyo, Shikkoku, were the biggest regional producers. This Iyo kasuri castle haba-ichi (one width) design (right) alternates with a chequered pattern. Another Iyo panel (second right) shows a turtle, representing longevity. Motifs included family crests, kanji characters, cherry and plum blossoms, pine, bamboo, folk tales and treasures – difficult to weave but easy to stitch.

Kasuri pattern arrangements

Gu-no-me (alternate pictorial and geometric patterns) designs also include haba-ni (two width) like this futon cover panel from San'in (above), with pine trees and knots. Smaller haba-san (three width) and haba-yon (four width) are woven for kimono. Chequerboard arrangements are familiar to quilters and are an effective way to combine sashiko with patchwork.

Fig 1 *Kotobuki* **character:** for the throw, enlarge on a photocopier by 135%.
Kotobuki **(good fortune):** Cursive and abstract forms of this kanji character are associated with special occasions such as weddings and New Year, but can be used for any happy occasion.

Fig 2 Pine tree: for the throw, enlarge on a photocopier by 135%; for the drawstring bag use at this size.
Matsu **(pine tree):** Pine is a symbol of longevity and endurance, as it is evergreen in the depths of winter, becoming gnarled with age. This pine motif is adapted from the San'in futon cover panel opposite.

Fig 3 Noshi: for the throw, enlarge on a photocopier by 135%.

Noshi: The name of the lucky bundle of dried abalone strips is a homonym for 'extend', hence its link to good fortune. *Noshi* are often represented by decorative fabric strips. Originally they were used to decorate gifts, a tradition that continues today.

Fig 4 Castle: for the throw, enlarge on a photocopier by 135%.

Shiro (castle): The central keep stands on a massive stone foundation wall, surrounded by pine trees. It is probably inspired by Matsuyama Castle, as *Iyo kasuri* was produced nearby. Matsuyama is one of the few castles in Japan remaining intact from the Edo era.

Fig 5 Koi carp: for the throw, enlarge on a photocopier by 135%.

Koi carp: The koi is a symbol of good fortune, associated with Boys' Day (now Children's Day) and a popular motif for boys' kimono. For more information about koi, see page 107.

Fig 6 Kiri paulownia crest: for the throw, enlarge on a photocopier by 135%.

Kiri: The famous paulownia *kamon* (family crest) originated in the Imperial Court during the late 8th century and was bestowed by the Emperor for loyal service. The right to use this crest has passed through various clans although the Tokugawa Shogunate preferred its own triple hollyhock crest. Today, it is often seen on rented *tomesode,* women's formal black kimono, as it may be used by anyone.

Tansu Pocket Hanging

Whether for your home office, your sewing equipment or a handy holder for the latest remote control, the pockets in this wall hanging are an unusual way to store bits and pieces. The subtle effect of shaded threads looks like *kakurezashi* (hidden sashiko), where the finished work was overdyed with indigo, so both thread and fabric became deep blue and the pattern was gradually revealed as they faded at different rates. Two *shippō* (seven treasures) variations from Shōnai district,

Yamagata, decorate the top two pockets. The bigger pocket combines four sashiko patterns, beginning with *shippō tsunagi* at the bottom, then two rows of *nowaki* ('grasses'), followed by two *seigaiha* (ocean wave) variations.

Tansu are chests of drawers (see page 85), ranging in size from large pieces of furniture to small boxes for personal items. The assorted drawer arrangements of small *tansu* and vintage sewing boxes inspired the pockets on this hanging.

Technique Taster

One of the *shippō* motifs on a smaller scale decorates this business card case, cleverly sewn and lined in one step! Use one side for your own cards and the other for useful contacts. Suitable for business cards up to 3½in x 2½in (8.9cm x 6.4cm). Instructions are overleaf.

I chose the mid blue fabric for this hanging to show the shaded thread to its best advantage – now you see the pattern, now you don't . . . The pocket hanging can be displayed on a short dowel or strip of wood. See page 86 for the instructions.

Business Card Case

Sashiko pattern used: *shippō* (seven treasures) variation
Finished size: 3¾in x 4¾in (9.5cm x 12cm) opened flat

You will need

- Cotton *tsumugi* or chambray
  4¼in x 8¼in (10.8cm x 21cm)
- Striped cotton 4¼in x 8¼in
  (10.8cm x 21cm)
- Medium sashiko thread, shaded
  blue to white
- Sewing thread
- Basic sewing and marking kit

Idea

Tsumugi is thinner and more finely woven than most sashiko fabrics, so it is less bulky. Indian shot cotton and silk noil are also suitable. Experiment with fabric oddments!

1 Marking the sashiko:

On the plain fabric, mark the pattern as shown in **Fig 1** below (see marking methods, page 21). Centre the design on the fabric and mark a 3½in (8.9cm) square grid and diagonal lines. Mark the large curves with a 3½in (8.9cm) diameter circle template. Mark the smaller central circle with a 2½in (6.4cm) diameter circle template.

2 Stitching the sashiko:

Stitch the central circle first and then stitch the first diagonal line, as shown by the red arrow, beginning at the red dot. Stitch the second diagonal line, then stitch the curves, as shown by the blue arrow, working around the motif. When stitching is finished, press.

Fig 1 Marking the *shippō* variation pattern.

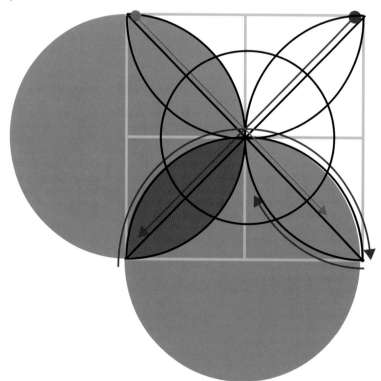

3 Assembling the card case:

With right sides together, machine sew the outer sashiko panel and lining together along one short side. Press this seam open, so the seam allowance lies back against the fabric. Press a ¼in (6mm) seam allowance under on the wrong side of the other short side of each piece but don't sew yet. On the wrong side draw a line 1½in (3.8cm) from each end of the panel, parallel to the ends. Use this as a guide and fold the whole strip as in **Fig 2**. The seamed end will be sandwiched inside the right fold, with the seam allowance folded back against itself. The open end will be sandwiched inside the left fold, with the end of the lining and the sashiko panel lined up and the pressed hems as shown. Line up the top edges all the way along and pin. Repeat for the bottom edge. Machine sew with a ¼in (6mm) seam.

4 Turn the card case right side out by pulling the fabric gently through the end opening between the two panels – it's like magic! Keep turning until you have pulled the pockets through. Make sure the corners are turned out well. Press and then slipstitch the gap closed. The picture below shows the case from the inside.

Fig 2 Assembling the case.

line up top edges, pin and sew and repeat for bottom edges

this line is drawn on the fabric

sashiko panel (wrong side)

this line is drawn on the fabric

Sashiko Inspirations

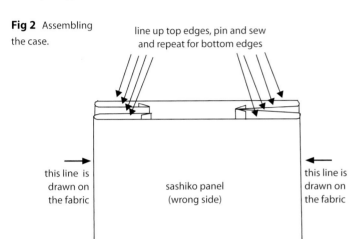

Tansu and haribako

Tansu (chests) come in all shapes and sizes. Haribako (literally 'needle boxes') have two styles, one with a tall post to hold a pincushion and kakehari clip (see page 14) and the other with a folding top containing a secret compartment. The two shown here are about 100 and 50 years old and are made of mulberry and cypress. Both have a slot for a ruler. The lighter cypress box has its original lacquered ruler (these are often missing from old boxes) marked in sun (Japanese inches – see page 18). The sashiko pocket hanging would be great to store your sewing items too.

Kakurezashi

Many old sashiko items have indigo thread, but in true kakurezashi (hidden sashiko) the whole piece has been dyed again after stitching, like this sorihikihappi (sled-hauling waistcoat) above. It creates a beautiful texture with subtle colour, as the thread and fabric fade at a different rate. Modern stitchers can use it for textural interest.

Pocket Hanging

Sashiko patterns used: *shippō* (seven treasures) variations, *shippō tsunagi* (linked seven treasures), *nowaki* (grasses), *seigaiha* (ocean waves) and variation
Finished size: 14½in x 11½in (36.8cm x 29.2cm)

Tip
Choose your thread first, then select your fabric shade. The darkest shade in the thread is not necessarily the one you like best for your background! You can use any shade that appears in the thread for the fabric, and the stitching will still shade in and out of the background.

You will need

- **Sashiko fabric:**
  one piece 8½in x 10½in (21.6cm x 26.7cm) for back of large pocket

  one piece 15½in x 10½in (39.4cm x 26.7cm) for front of large pocket

  two pieces 5½in x 5¼in (14cm x 13.3cm) for back of small pockets

  two pieces 8½in x 5¼in (21.6cm x 13.3cm) for front of small pockets

- **Cotton *tsumugi* or a dark plain cotton:**
  one piece 5½in x 1in (14cm x 2.5cm) for between small pockets

  one piece 10½in x 1in (26.7cm x 2.5cm) for between small and large pockets

  two pieces 14in x 1½in (35.6cm x 3.8cm) for vertical borders

  two pieces 12½in x 1½in (31.8cm x 3.8cm) for horizontal borders

  one piece 16in x 12½in (40.6cm x 31.8cm) for backing

- **Plain cotton strip 12in x 3in (30.5cm x 7.6cm), for a hanging sleeve**

- **Medium sashiko thread, shaded blue to white**

- **Sewing thread**

- **Basic sewing and marking kit**

1 Marking the sashiko:

Zigzag or overlock the edges of the sashiko panels. Take the 8½in x 5¼in (21.6cm x 13.3cm) pieces for the two top pockets and fold each one in half and press to form the pocket. Draw a 4in (10.2cm) square in the centre of each pocket, with the top of the square on the pressed fold (**Fig 1**).

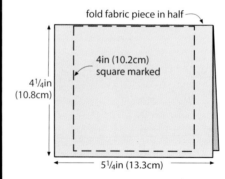

fold fabric piece in half

4in (10.2cm) square marked

4¼in (10.8cm)

5¼in (13.3cm)

Fig 1 For the two top pockets, fold the fabric in half and mark a 4in (10.2cm) square.

Draw lines at 2in (5cm) intervals, quartering each square. Draw diagonal lines on each square. Now mark the two *shippō* variations, following **Fig 2** (right-hand pocket) and **Fig 3** (left-hand pocket). Mark the pattern in Fig 2 using a 4in (10.2cm) diameter circle to mark the interlocking semicircles and a 3in (7.6cm) circle for the inner circle.

Mark the pattern in Fig 3, beginning with a 4in (10.2cm) circle centred on the square. Mark a 1in (2.5cm) circle in the centre, as a guideline for the curved points. Use a 5½in (14cm) diameter circle template to mark the curved points, linking the outer circle to the inner circle, as shown.

Fig 2 The *shippō* variation pattern for the top right-hand pocket.

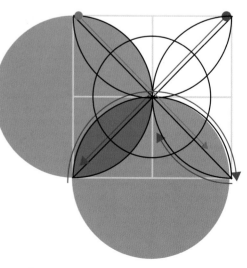

Fig 3 The *shippō* (seven treasures) variation pattern for the top left-hand pocket.

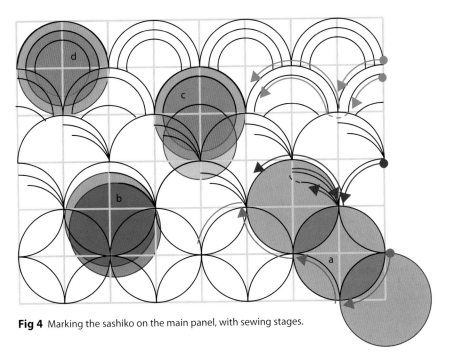

Fig 4 Marking the sashiko on the main panel, with sewing stages.

2 To mark the main sashiko panel, fold the 15½in x 10½in (39.4cm x 26.7cm) fabric piece in half and press to form the pocket. Mark the patterns as **Fig 4**. Draw a 1½in (3.2cm) grid in the centre of the pocket, with the top line of the grid on the pressed fold. Starting from the bottom of the grid and using a 2½in (6.4cm) diameter circle template, mark *shippō tsunagi* (**a**) over two rows by drawing overlapping circles.

Mark *nowaki* (**b**) by drawing semicircles, offset over two rows, adding the 'grasses' inside each semicircle, pivoting the circle template at the corner of each semicircle. Continue marking the offset semicircles to the top of the grid.

Complete the *seigaiha* variation pattern (**c**) by marking a second semicircle in each, using a 2in (5cm) diameter circle template, and adding a shallow arc at the bottom of that pattern using the same template.

Complete *seigaiha* (**d**) across the top row with a 2in (5cm) circle and 1½in (3.8cm) circle.

3 Stitching the sashiko:

Open out the folded pocket panels and stitch through only one layer. Stitch the pattern in Fig 2 (right-hand pocket) by stitching the vertical, horizontal and diagonal lines first, crossing the centre. Stitch around the large circle, then stitch the curved points, as indicated by the red arrows.

Stitch the pattern in Fig 3 (left-hand pocket) by stitching the first diagonal line, as shown by the red arrow. Stitch the second diagonal line, as shown by blue arrow, then semicircles, working around the motif. Stitch the circle, and then press.

4 Begin stitching the larger pocket panel with the *shippō* section, at the bottom of the panel, following the red arrows in Fig 4, stitching in diagonal wavy lines. Next stitch the *nowaki* section, following the blue arrows, stitch across each semicircle and along the grasses, stranding across the back between the grasses as shown by the dashed blue line. Stitch *seigaiha* and its variation following the green arrows, stitching the outer semicircle first, then filling in the smaller semicircles, and stranding across the back as shown by the dashed green line. Press when finished.

5 Making the patchwork:

Arrange the folded sashiko panels on the front of the remaining pieces, as in **Fig 5**, lining up the bottom edges of the pocket with the edge of the panel and pinning.

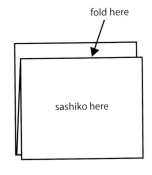

Fig 5 Arranging the folded sashiko panels.

6 Assemble the patchwork as in **Fig 6**. With a ¼in (6mm) seam allowance, machine sew the 5½in x 1in (14cm x 2.5cm) strip to the left side of the left top pocket. Press all seams towards the narrow strips. Sew to the other top pocket. Sew the 10½in x 1in (26.7cm x 2.5cm) strip to the top of the largest pocket. Sew the two panel halves together. Add side borders first, then top and bottom borders.

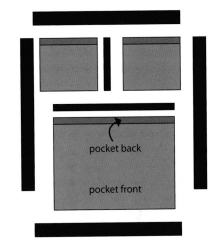

Fig 6 Sewing the patchwork pieces together.

7 Finishing the hanging:

Place the front panel and backing fabric right sides together and pin all round. Machine sew with a ½in (1.3cm) seam allowance, leaving a 4in (10.2cm) gap at the centre of the lower edge. Trim off the corners within the seam allowance, but do not cut right up to the stitches – to about ⅛in (3mm). Turn the hanging right way out through the gap, easing out corners. Lay the panel flat and smooth. Turn under the raw edges at the bottom, pin or tack and slipstitch the gap closed. From the back, hand sew right round the panel ⅛in (3mm) from the edge with small stitches through backing and seam allowances only to keep the backing in place.

8 Making a hanging sleeve:

Using the remaining strip, turn under the ends and hem. With *wrong* sides together, fold in half lengthwise and machine sew. Don't turn the sleeve inside out – the seam will be hidden when sewn to the hanging. Press the sleeve flat, with the seam open and centred along one side. Pin the sleeve to the back of the hanging, ½in (1.3cm) from the top edge and centred. The sleeve will be shorter than the hanging. Hand sew the sleeve to the hanging, keeping stitches invisible from the front.

Kiku Panel

Japanese designers often fill in the outline of a large motif with another smaller pattern, varying the densities of the patterns. My *kiku* (chrysanthemum) panel opposite uses three *hitomezashi* (one-stitch sashiko) patterns to achieve this effect – *komezashi* (rice stitch) and a variation alternated for the petals, plus *kikkōzashi* (tortoiseshell stitch) in the centre, using shaded threads within a double outline. It is more challenging to stitch *hitomezashi* inside another shape than stitching it in a square, but the

regular petals repeat the same outline. The lively fronds filling the corners are *karakusa* designs adapted from *katazome* stencilled fabrics and *tsutsugaki*, freehand rice paste resist dyeing.

Tsutsugaki cloths, such as *furoshiki* wrapping cloths, often used a large *kamon* crest or floral motif at the centre, filling out the corners with *karakusa*. The tranquil, densely stitched, formal *kiku* centre contrasts with the lighter feeling of the scrolling, organic corner designs.

Technique Taster

A single chrysanthemum outline on this box lid has just enough space to try out the two *komezashi* designs in green and cream threads. It could also be used for a greetings card, a sachet or as a single sampler motif. See instructions overleaf.

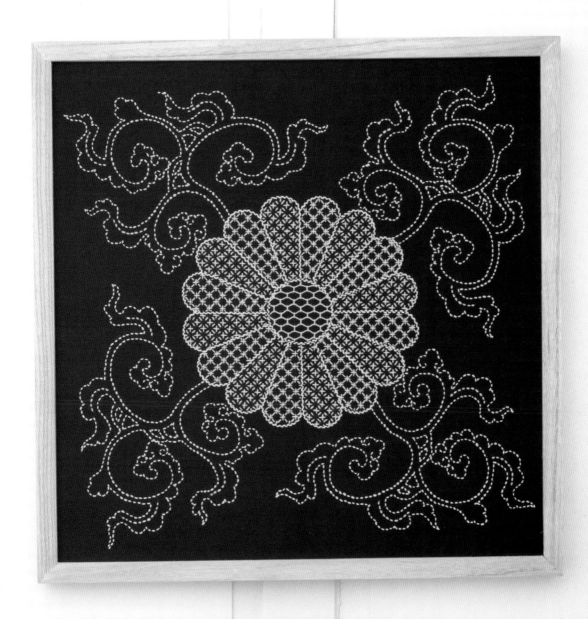

The *kiku* panel has details on each *karakusa* scroll stitched in ice blue thread, co-ordinating with the shaded blue thread for the central motif. White and shades of indigo are the main colours used for *tsutsugaki*. The design could be used for a striking quilt centre. See page 92 for instructions.

Chrysanthemum Box

Sashiko patterns used: *komezashi* (rice stitch) and variation
Finished size: 3in (7.6cm) motif diameter

You will need

- **Sashiko fabric 6¼in x 4¼in (15.9cm x 10.8cm)**
- **Fine sashiko thread in cream and medium sashiko thread in light green**
- **Medium-weight iron-on interfacing 6¼in x 4¼in (15.9cm x 10.8cm)**
- **Basic sewing and marking kit**
- **Thin card for template**
- **Box with 6in x 4in (15.2cm x 10.2cm) lid aperture**

Tip
Boxes with photo display lids are great for this project, but make sure the sashiko can be fitted into the box easily. Sashiko panels are thicker than photo paper, so they won't slide into narrow display slots. Lids with removable backings, like photo frames, are easier to use.

1 Marking the sashiko:
Mark horizontal and vertical lines through the centre of the sashiko fabric, quartering it. Make a template using the quarter flower in **Fig 1**. Line this up on the crossed lines, and mark the flower outline, a quarter at a time. Starting from the crossed lines, mark horizontal and vertical lines ³⁄₁₆in (5mm) apart.

Fig 1 Use this actual size quarter flower outline to make a template and transfer the shape to your fabric.

Tip
Remember that standard metric sizes for photo frames are not the exact equivalent of imperial sizes – the standard imperial size for a box like this is 6in x 4in but the metric size would be 15cm x 10cm, slightly smaller all round. Make sure you trim your panel to fit the actual size of your box.

2 Stitching the sashiko:
Stitch around the motif using fine cream sashiko thread. Following **Fig 2** and **Fig 3** opposite, stitch the first two stages of *komezashi* – *yokogushi* (horizontal rows) and *jūjizashi* ('10' cross stitch). Half the motif is completed with the first stage of *komezashi*, in **Fig 4**, while the other half is finished as the *komezashi* variation, **Fig 5**. See *hitomezashi* stitching tips on page 27.

3 Finishing the box:
Press the completed sashiko. Following the manufacturer's instructions, iron the piece of interfacing to the back. Check the size of the box aperture and trim the panel to fit exactly – in this case, 6in x 4in (15.2cm x 10.2cm) – and insert the panel.

Fig 2 *Yokogushi* **(horizontal rows):**
this is the basic *hitomezashi* stitch. Stitch back and forth across the grid. The position of the stitches and gaps alternates between one row and the next. Accurate base rows are important – the stitches should go exactly across one grid square, on the horizontal line.

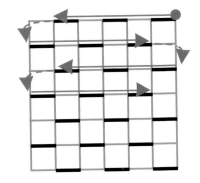
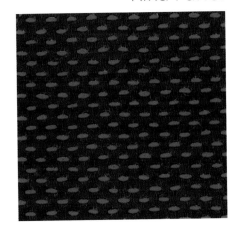

Fig 3 *Jūjizashi* **('10' cross stitch):**
this stitch is so-called because it looks like the *kanji* character '10'. Stitch a second set of stitches, crossing over the *yokogushi* stitches at right angles. Note there is no grid line to guide these – just line them up by eye. This is one of a few *hitomezashi* patterns where the stitches cross, creating an interesting texture. The stitches are shown in two different colours to show the pattern sequence more clearly.

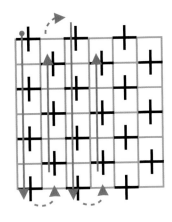

Fig 4 *Komezashi* **(rice stitch):**
this stitch is so-called because it looks like the *kanji* character for 'rice'. Stitch extra diagonal lines, taking a small stitch behind each cross from the previous stitch pattern. Usually, all the diagonal stitches leaning in one direction are completed and then the diagonal stitches are added in the other direction, stitching in complete rows, but for this project, only one diagonal line is stitched.

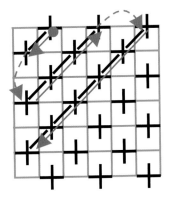
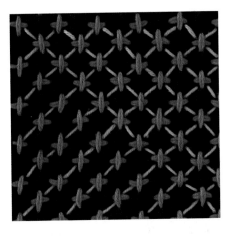

Fig 5 *Kawari komezashi* **(rice stitch variation):** *kawari* means 'variation' and here the diagonal lines of stitches are placed between the crosses, rather than linking the cross centres.

Idea
Try filling in the flower centre with different stitch combinations – try *jūjizashi* and *kawari komezashi* or *yokogushi* and *kikkōzashi* (page 93).

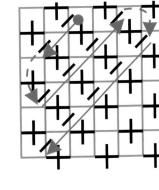

Kiku Panel

Sashiko patterns used: *kikkōzashi* (tortoiseshell stitch), *komezashi* (rice stitch) and variation
Finished size: to fit a 20in (50.8cm) square frame

1 **Marking the sashiko:**
Zigzag or overlock the edges of the panel before you begin. Mark horizontal and vertical lines through the centre of the sashiko fabric, quartering it, as shown by the red dashed lines in **Fig 1** below. Now make a template using the quarter flower pattern given in

Fig 2 opposite. Line this up on the crossed lines on your fabric and mark the flower outline, a quarter at a time. Mark a 2½in (6.4cm) diameter circle in the centre. Mark the petals, starting from the crossed lines, mark horizontal and vertical lines ¼in (6mm) apart, all over the flower motif.

You will need

- **Sashiko fabric 22in (55.9cm) square**
- **Medium sashiko thread in cream and ice blue**
- **Basic sewing and marking kit**
- **Thin card for template**
- **Frame and backing board, with 20in (50.8cm) square aperture**
- **Strong thread to lace sashiko over frame panel**

Idea
Using fabric with a ¼in (6mm) or ⅛in (3mm) check would remove the need for marking the hitomezashi guidelines, using the check to line up the stitches instead.

Fig 1 This diagram shows the overall design as it will eventually look on the fabric. Begin by marking the sashiko fabric into quarters following the dashed red lines.

2 Trace or photocopy the *karakusa* corner motif from **Fig 3** overleaf. Using the Chaco paper transfer method from page 21, transfer the design to each corner of the panel, using Fig 1 as a guide. The solid red lines indicate approximately the edge of each motif area. Note that the motifs do not line up with the central dashed red lines, but are offset. Remember to leave an unmarked edge of about 1¾in (4.4cm) all around the design to allow for framing. Draw over the Chaco lines with another marker, if you wish.

3 Stitching the sashiko:

Start stitching the sashiko with the flower outlines in cream, with a double row of running stitch to give a bold effect (see pictures below). Stitch the first row of stitches on the marked line, making sure the gap is about half the length of the stitch. Stitch the second row close to the first, staggering the stitches so that the new stitches overlap the gap. Stitch the scrolling motifs in outline with cream thread, adding the inner line detail after in ice blue.

4 Using a single strand of shaded blue thread, fill in the flower, stitching *yokogushi* (horizontal rows), following Fig 2 on page 91, then filling in the petals only with *jūjizashi* ('10' cross stitch), following Fig 3 on page 91. Complete alternate petals with *komezashi* (rice stitch) and *kawari komezashi* (rice stitch variation), following **Fig 4** below and **Fig 5** on page 91. This time, stitch the second set of diagonal rows for *komezashi*. Following Fig 4, complete the flower centre with *kikkōzashi* (tortoiseshell stitch). Press when finished.

These two pictures show details of some of the different patterns.

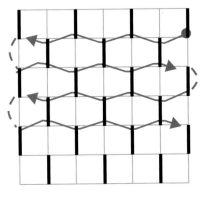

Fig 4 *Kikkōzashi*: this pattern is based on a *yokogushi* foundation, with the extra 'stitches' simply threaded through the first stitches. The only time the thread goes through the fabric is at the beginning and end of each row, where it goes under the *yokogushi* stitch. Follow the red zigzag lines for the threading sequence. Start and finish the threaded section with a simple knot on the back of the work. Strand across the back from one row to the next, making sure you have enough thread to go right across the row without a break.

5 Framing the panel:

To frame your panel, refer to the advice on page 27 or take your work to a professional framer who will have a selection of frames.

Fig 2 Quarter flower template (actual size) for marking out the flower outline: position your template where the dashed red lines cross, mark the quarter shape and then turn through 90 degrees to mark the second segment, and so on.

Fig 3 The *karakusa* scrolling corner motif (actual size): transfer the design on to your fabric with reference to step 2 and Fig 1.

Idea

To use the design for a larger panel or quilt centre, the pattern here can be repeated for a corner infill design, placing the left part of the scroll into the panel corner and extending the stem to the panel edge.

Sashiko Inspirations

Karakusa, katazome and tsutsugaki

Scrolling karakusa motifs were introduced from China around 1,500 years ago, and the name is written by combing the kanji characters kara for 'China' and kusa, 'plant' or 'grass'. Originally it represented honeysuckle, but quickly developed into an abstract, scrolling arabesque, sometimes with hōsōge, an imaginary flower based on the peony. Early designs included birds, butterflies and karyōbinga, heavenly beings like angels. At first, karakusa was a pattern for the aristocracy but its lavish scrolling designs were perfect for the tsutsugaki freehand paste-resist dyeing technique, becoming a popular design for household textiles in bridal trousseaux. It also became a mainstay of katazome stencil-dyed fabrics, like the early 20th century fabrics shown here. Various shades of indigo were the most popular, but touches of madder red, ochre and green were sometimes added after the indigo dyebath. The pattern is occasionally found on old sashiko, like the furoshiki detail shown centre right.

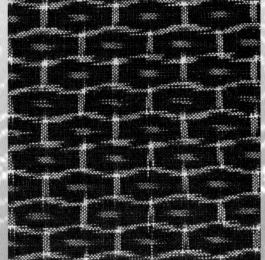

Komon

Small patterns or komon are often used to fill in larger motifs, such as geometric or floral outlines, as well as being used as all-over patterns. They may be stencilled, embroidered or woven, like the kasuri version of the kikkō pattern shown right. As many geometric komon designs have hitomezashi versions, this is also very effective in sashiko and the varying density of the patterns can be used to create light and dark tones.

Ranru Wall Hanging

The subtle colours of a bundle of Indian shot cotton quilting scraps gave me the idea of combining them with sashiko in a patchwork wall hanging. The mixture of squares and rectangles looks like vintage *ranru* (tatter) cloths, an ingenious method of patching and re-using old scraps. Classic sashiko patterns like *raimon* (spiral) and *masuzashi* (square measure sashiko) were routinely resized to fit the proportions of old work jackets, so I resized them to fit the patchwork pieces – simple but unusual. *Asanoha* (hemp leaf) is another pattern often seen in a distorted version, so I added that too. The striped fabric I used has simple rows of stitching, sashiko in its most utilitarian form, used here to enhance the woven stripe.

Backing the patchwork panel with muslin before stitching the sashiko stops the edges fraying while you sew. Many household items were made from *ranru* fabrics. The subtle shades of faded old fabric and their asymmetry are part of their charm.

Technique Taster

Asanoha is resized to fit the panel on the side of this handy tote bag. Strips frame the scrap of sashiko fabric that was my starting point. The bottom corners of the bag are shaped to give it depth. It's a simple classic that you'll want to make more than once. Instructions overleaf.

The largest and darkest patches in the wall hanging define the top-left and bottom-right corners, while the other corners both have brighter ochre patches. As there is more than one patch in several sizes, experiment with different colour arrangements before sewing. See page 100 for instructions.

Tote Bag

Sashiko patterns used: *asanoha* (hemp leaf) variation
Finished size: 15in x 12in (38.1cm x 30.5cm)

You will need

- **Sashiko fabric 10½in x 7½in (26.7cm x 19cm)**
- **Thick cotton fabric:**
  one strip 18½in x 13in (47cm x 33cm)
  one strip 3¼in x 13in (8.3cm x 33cm)
  two strips 10½in x 3¼in (26.7cm x 8.3cm)
  two strips 13in x 4in (33cm x 10.2cm) for handles
- **Plain cotton 31in x 13in (78.7cm x 33cm) for lining**
- **Sewing thread**
- **Basic sewing and marking kit**

Tip
If your piece of sashiko fabric is slightly smaller, resize the outer patchwork panel. Make a sketch to note down the new fabric sizes. Use the finished outer panel as a pattern to cut the lining.

1 Marking and stitching:
Zigzag or overlock all the patchwork pieces before you begin. Mark a rectangle on the sashiko fabric ½in (1.3cm) inside all the edges. Following **Fig 1**, quarter the rectangle equally into four smaller rectangles, then equally again into eight rectangles. Mark zigzag lines, as shown by the heavy black lines in diagrams c and d. Stitch the sashiko, following the red arrows in c, d, and e. Refer to the stitching tips on page 26. Press the completed panel.

2 Assembling the patchwork:
Machine sew the patchwork, as shown in **Fig 2**, using ¼in (6mm) seams throughout. Sew the two 10½in x 3¼in (26.7cm x 8.3cm) strips to either side of the sashiko panel and press towards the strips. Sew the largest piece to one end of the patchwork and the 13in x 3¼in (33cm x 8.3cm) strip to the other end and press.

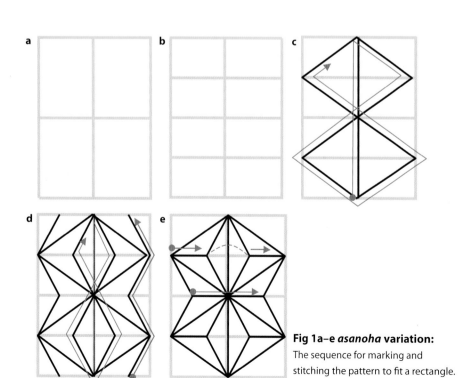

Fig 1a–e *asanoha* variation:
The sequence for marking and stitching the pattern to fit a rectangle.

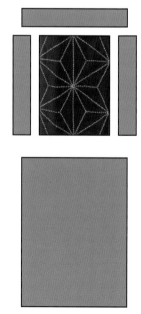

Fig 2 Sewing the patchwork pieces together.

3 Making the handles:

Follow step 6 and Fig 5 on page 60 to make the bag handles.

4 Assembling the bag:

Temporarily fold the bag panel in half, right sides outside, so the top of the bag meets. Arrange the handles on the right side of the bag panel as shown in **Fig 3**, allowing the handle ends to overlap the edge of the bag panel by 1/2in (1.3cm). Repeat for the back of the bag. The gap between the handle ends is 4in (10.2cm) on each side. Make sure the handles are the same length and not twisted. Tack (baste) in place.

Fig 3 Positioning the bag handles on the front of the bag. Repeat for the back of the bag.

Fig 4 Sewing up the sides of the bag.

5

With the bag panel folded right sides together and using a 1/2in (1.3cm) seam, machine sew down the sides of the bag, shown by the dashed lines in **Fig 4**. Clip the corners within the seam allowance but don't cut right up to the stitches – leave about 1/8in (3mm). Press the side seams open.

6

Make the lining by folding the lining fabric in half, right sides together and, with a 1/2in (1.3cm) seam, machine sew down both sides, as shown in **Fig 5**. Leave a 4in (10.2cm) gap unsewn in the second side. The bag will be turned right side out through the unsewn gap. Press the seams open.

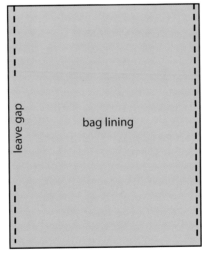

Fig 5 Making the bag lining.

7

Turn the outer bag section right side out. Keeping the bag lining turned inside out, place the bag outer inside the lining, aligning the top edge and the side seams. Machine sew around the top of the bag, sewing the lining to the bag outer all round with a 1/2in (1.3cm) seam. Turn the bag right side out, through the unsewn gap in the lining side seam. Press the seam at the top of the bag. Machine or hand sew around the top of the bag, about 1/8in (3mm) from the edge. Turn the bag inside out and slipstitch the gap in the lining closed.

Idea

The *raimon* (spiral) and *masuzashi* (square measure sashiko) designs overleaf also adapt easily to fit this bag panel – so why not make a set of bags?

8

Push the bottom corners of the lining into the bottom corners of the bag. Tack (baste) the lining to the outside of the bag for about 4in (10.2cm) at the bottom corners. Fold the corners to make a point, as shown in **Fig 6**. Mark a line at right angles to the seam, 2in (5cm) from the point, then pin and machine sew across, sewing the bottom corner of the bag and lining together and creating a triangular flap of fabric. Fold this flap up against the side seam and use sashiko stitches to stitch the flap to the bag, 1/4in (6mm) from the edge, sewing right through the lining. To finish, slipstitch the edges of the flap to the bag to neaten.

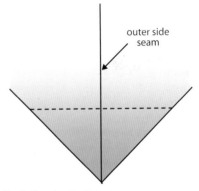

Fig 6 Creating the bag corners.

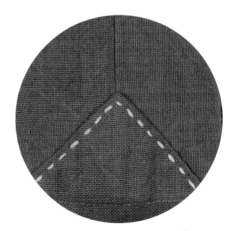

Sewing across the bottom corners and then folding up and sewing the triangle of fabric creates the corners of the bag.

Ranru Hanging

Sashiko patterns used: *asanoha* (hemp leaf) variation, *raimon* (spiral) and *masuzashi* (square measure sashiko)

Finished size: 38in x 24in (96.5cm x 61cm)

You will need

- **Indian shot cotton, *tsumugi* or similar in various colours:**

  two pieces 10½in x 8½in (26.7cm x 21.6cm) (A)

  two squares 8½in (21.6cm) (B)

  three pieces 8½in x 6½in (21.6cm x 16.5cm) (C)

  two squares 6½in (16.5cm) (D)

  two pieces 8½in x 4½in (21.6cm x 11.4cm) (E)

  one piece 6½in x 4½in (16.5cm x 11.4cm) (F)

  one square 4½in (11.4cm) (G)

- **Two striped cotton squares 6½in (16.5cm) (H)**

- **Very narrow striped cotton for border:**

  two strips 24½in x 2½in (62.2cm x 6.4cm)

  two strips 34½in x 2½in (87.6cm x 6.4cm)

- **Plain cotton:**
  38½in x 24½in (96.5cm x 62.2cm) for backing
  24in x 8in (61cm x 20.3cm) for hanging sleeve

- **Muslin 38½in x 24½in (96.5cm x 62.2cm) for wadding (batting)**

- **Fine cream sashiko thread 170 metre skein**

- **Sewing thread**

- **Basic sewing and marking kit**

Idea

The patchwork centre, 34in x 20in (86.4cm x 50.8cm), can be repeated and treated as a giant rectangular quilt block – six panels would make a quilt centre 68in x 60in (172.7cm x 152.4cm).

1 Making the patchwork:

Lay out the patchwork pieces, using **Fig 1** as a guide. The patches are labelled with letters in the You Will Need list. Machine sew patches together in pairs and strips, as indicated on the diagram using ¼in (6mm) seams throughout, pinning each seam as you go. For the final patchwork assembly, you will need to only partly sew some seams. Begin by sewing the striped square (H) to the bottom of the centre patchwork strip (B, B), but sewing only 3in (7.6cm). Press the seam towards the centre strip. Add the strip of squares on the left (D, C, C) to the centre patchwork strip and sew the whole seam. From now on, press all new seams towards the piece you just added. Add the patchwork piece at the top of the panel. Add the right strip (F, H, C, D). Add the bottom strip (G, E). Add the bottom right patch (A). Now go back to the first seam that was only partly sewn and finish sewing it, overlapping the end of your previous stitches by about ½in (1.3cm). Press this seam towards the middle of the panel. Add the side borders next, then the top and bottom borders. Press towards the outside of the panel.

2 Marking the sashiko:

Using the photograph on page 20 as a guide, **Fig 2** and **Fig 3** opposite and **Fig 1a–e** on page 98, mark the *raimon*, *masuzashi* and *asanoha* patterns in the relevant squares. Spaces between lines for *raimon* and *masuzashi* is ½in (1.3cm). Use a quilters' ruler with parallel lines to mark the patterns. Start by drawing lines parallel to the sides of the

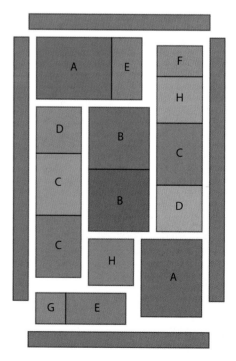

Fig 1 Layout of all the patchwork pieces.

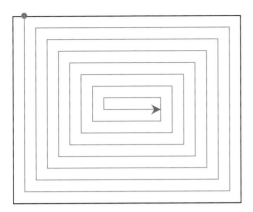

Fig 2 _raimon_ spiral: mark the pattern beginning at the dot and following the direction of the red arrow.

Fig 3 _masuzashi_: mark the pattern following the red arrows.

with a ¼in (6mm) seam allowance, leaving an 8in (20.3cm) gap at the centre of the lower edge. Trim off the corners within the seam allowance, to about ⅛in (3mm) of the stitches. Turn through to the right side and ease the corners out so they are sharp. Lay the panel out flat and smooth. Turn under the raw edges at the bottom, pin or tack (baste) and slipstitch the gap closed. From the back, hand sew right round the panel ⅛in (3mm) from the edge with small stitches through backing and seam allowances only to keep the backing in place.

5 Making a hanging sleeve:
Follow step 8 on page 87 for making a hanging sleeve.

Tip
Hang the wall hanging from a wood batten the same length as the sleeve – 1in x ½in (2.5cm x 1.3cm) wood section is fine. Screw a mirror plate to each end and screw this to the wall. The hanging will hide the mirror plates.

patch and work inwards. Draw _asanoha_ following instructions on page 98. Tack the patchwork panel to the muslin (see page 22).

3 Stitching the sashiko:
Raimon: stitch the pattern in a spiral following the direction of the red arrow.
Masuzashi: stitch the pattern from the outer square inwards, following the red arrow. Cross the corners by one stitch and strand across the back to turn the corner, as indicated in the diagram by a red dashed line.
Asanoha: stitch the pattern following Fig 1 on page 98. Press the panel when complete.

4 Making up the wall hanging:
Place the front panel and backing fabric right sides together and pin all round. Machine sew

---

Sashiko Inspirations

Ranru and _boromono_ cloths
Cloths pieced from recycled scraps have become very collectable in recent years, as people appreciate their abstract qualities. Ranru means 'tatter' and boromono means 'rag thing'. They were part of everyday life for frugal farmers and working families until the mid 20th century. As people became more prosperous many ranru were thrown away. Fabrics included stripes, checks and kasuri ikat as well as plain indigo cotton. Simple sashiko, in straight lines or spirals, was often added to reinforce and strengthen fabrics. Some of these cloths were made from patchwork while others were appliqué patches. The technique was used for bedding, table covers, rugs and drapes for chests of drawers. Many were intended to be seen in use from the plainer side, with the patchwork on the reverse, rather like some vintage Welsh wholecloth quilts with patchwork backs, so it is ironic that the patchwork is the side most valued today. Ranru are a wonderful resource for studying old Japanese fabrics.

Ranru noragi
The ranru technique was also used for work clothes. Again, the inside is often more interesting and more heavily pieced than the outside. The jacket above has simple sashiko in blue thread following the stripes on the outer body fabric. Patches on the outside of the jacket are arranged in a more symmetrical layout than the inside, where there was little attempt to match one side to the other. Because these linings are often more intricately pieced and patched from smaller scraps, collectors tend to display these jackets turned inside out.

Koi Scroll

This chapter shows how to use coloured sashiko to create beautiful pictorial designs, which can be as simple or intricate as you like. A *kakejiku* (scroll) is an indispensable decoration for a traditional room in Japan and is changed according to the season and occasion. A pair of magnificent koi carp swim down this one, among gentle ripples of water. A single koi image has been used but the impact of the pictorial design is increased by mirror imaging this to create a second fish, giving fluidity and movement to the piece.

Blue silk obi brocade provided the arrangement for the koi while a Katsushika Hokusai illustration was used as inspiration for the koi details. Their outlines are stitched with a doubled thread but their scales and fins use single thread for a lighter effect, using coloured and shaded threads. The scroll border is added with simple patchwork. A thin strip of wood keeps the top straight and a dowel weights the bottom.

Technique Taster

Greetings cards are ideal for small pictorial sashiko samples, allowing you to practice the technique and also experiment with different thread and fabric colour combinations. These two cards feature a maple leaf and a simple flower – both easy to stitch but so stylish and effective. See overleaf for instructions.

The scroll here uses a blue, cream and orange colour scheme but there are numerous named varieties of ornamental koi, including solid colours, metallic scales and variegated shades, so there are many other colour possibilities for your scroll. See page 106 for the scroll instructions.

Greetings Cards

Sashiko patterns used: *momiji* (maple) and *kiku* (chrysanthemum)
Finished size of sashiko: 4in (10.2in) approximately

You will need (for each card)

- One piece of blue sashiko fabric, 4in (10.2cm) square
- Medium sashiko thread – oddments in various colours
- Tracing paper and card for templates
- Card blank with 3in (7.6cm) diameter or square aperture
- Double-sided adhesive tape and masking tape
- Basic sewing and marking kit

Idea
Cards are great projects for using up oddments or trying out new thread and fabric combinations.

1 Marking the sashiko:

Use the inside of the card aperture as a stencil to mark the working area on your fabric. Trace off or photocopy the motifs in **Fig 1** and **Fig 2** and stick the tracing paper to the card. When dry, cut out the template. Mark the designs, using the templates and the photographs as guides.

2 Stitching the sashiko:

With a doubled thread, stitch the leaf outline, water swirl and chrysanthemum petal outlines, starting and finishing with a knot (see page 23). Use a single thread to stitch the leaf veins and the extra lines down the flower petals.

Fig 1 *Momiji* (maple) template (actual size).

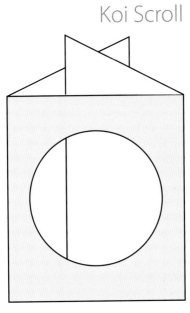

Fig 3 Double-fold card blank.

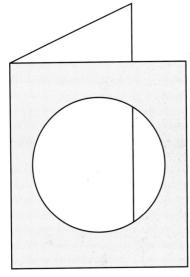

3 Mounting into a card:

Open out the card blank, arrange the sashiko behind the card aperture and use masking tape to hold it in place. If you are using a double-fold card blank as shown in **Fig 3**, the extra fold will hide the back of the sashiko. If your card has a single fold, shown in **Fig 4**, use a piece of paper and double-sided tape to cover the back of the sashiko neatly.

Tip

If you create a sashiko travel kit you will always have something to hand ready to stitch. Pack a small bag (like the drawstring bag on page 76) with 4in (10.2cm) squares of fabric with the designs marked, oddments of sashiko thread, a needle and a pair of scissors.

Fig 4 Single-fold card blank.

Fig 2 *Kiku* (chrysanthemum) template (actual size).

Koi Scroll

Sashiko pattern used: koi carp design
Finished size: 38½in x 12in (97.8cm x 30.5cm)

You will need

- Piece of cream sashiko fabric, 8½in x 20in (21.6cm x 50.8cm)
- Piece of muslin, 8½in x 20in (21.6cm x 50.8cm) (optional)
- Two strips of oriental patchwork fabric, 8½in x 1in (21.6cm x 2.5cm)
- Border fabric:
  two pieces 21in x 2½in (53.3cm x 6.4cm)
  one square 12½in (31.8cm)
  one piece 8½in x 12½in (21.6cm x 31.8cm)
- Backing fabric, 39½in x 12½in (100.4cm x 31.8cm), slightly shorter than panel
- Piece of muslin (optional), 8½in x 20in (21.6cm x 50.8cm)
- Medium sashiko thread in rust, persimmon and shaded blues
- Wooden dowel, 13½in (34.3cm) long x ⅝in (1.6cm) diameter
- Flat wood, ⅜in x ¼in x 13½in (1cm x 0.6cm x 34.3cm) approx
- Fine cord 18in (45.7cm)
- Sewing thread to match fabrics
- Tracing paper for template
- Chaco paper (blue)
- Adhesive tape
- Basic sewing and marking kit

1 Marking the sashiko:

Trace or photocopy the koi design from **Fig 1** overleaf. You will also need a mirror image for the koi at the top of the scroll – the tracing can be flipped over for this or ask for a mirror image at the copy shop. Arrange the two tracings or copies as shown in **Fig 2** and stick together with adhesive tape. Using the blue Chaco paper, transfer the pattern to the cream fabric, centring the pattern on the fabric (see marking fabric using Chaco paper, page 21). Overlock or zigzag the edges before you begin. Tack (baste) the sashiko fabric to the muslin (optional).

2 Stitching the sashiko:

With a doubled thread, stitch the koi outlines and the water swirls. Use a single thread to stitch the scale and fin details. The lower koi outline is stitched in rust, with the scales and fins in persimmon, but the upper koi is stitched entirely in persimmon. The picture on page 109 shows the stitching details of the lower koi actual size, so use this for reference. Rinse the sashiko if necessary to remove the Chaco marks and then.

Tip
Add extra dimension to the koi by layering the panel with polyester wadding after stitching the sashiko and quilting by hand or machine just outside the koi outlines. Trim the wadding almost to the panel edge.

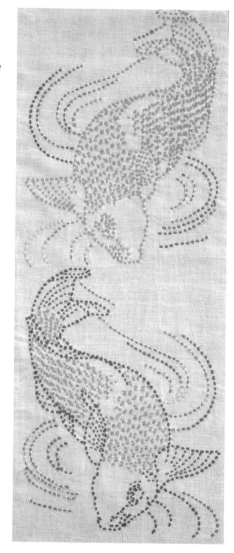

Fig 2 Trace a second koi as a mirror image of the bottom fish by flipping the tracing over, so the design looks like this.

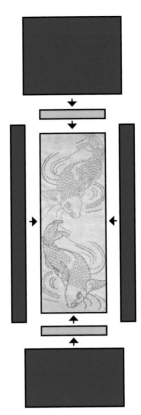

Fig 3 Layout of the scroll fabric pieces.

3 Making up the scroll:
With right sides together and using **Fig 3**, machine sew the two 8½in x 1in (21.6cm x 2.5cm) strips to the top and bottom of the panel. Press all seams outwards, as you go. Machine sew the two 21in x 2½in (53.3cm x 6.4cm) strips to the sides. Sew the 12½in (31.8cm) square to the top and the 8½in x 12½in (21.6cm x 31.8cm) piece to the bottom. Sew the backing fabric to the scroll across the bottom edge.

4 With right sides together, sew the sides of the scroll to the sides of the backing fabric, leaving about 1in (2.5cm) unsewn at the bottom for the dowel – check your dowel will go through this gap. The backing is slightly shorter than the scroll, so the scroll border fabric will wrap around the dowel towards the backing by ¾in (1.9cm). Turn right side out and press.

5 From the back, hand sew down each side, ⅛in (3mm) from the edge, with small, neat stitches, through backing and seam allowances only, to keep the backing in place. Turn in the raw edges along the top of the scroll and slipstitch the gap closed. Turn over the top of the scroll towards the backing fabric to make a channel for the flat wood strip hanger to go through. Check the wood will go through the channel, and then slipstitch in place. Push the wood hanger through the channel and tie the cord to the ends. You could hang scroll weights on the ends of the dowel – see below.

Idea
For a traditional finishing touch, make your own *fuchin* (scroll weights) to hang on the dowel, using a tassel topped with a large bead and loop (see picture, right).

Sashiko Inspirations

Beautiful koi
Hokusai's image of the bodhisattva Kannon riding on a giant carp (from the 13th volume of his Manga series) provided the detail for my sashiko koi. Carp are a symbol of good luck and are an unusual motif for kimono and obi, as seen on the mid-20th century woven obi brocade below. According to an old Chinese legend, when a carp finishes climbing the waterfall of the Dragon Gate of the Yellow River, it will be transformed into a dragon, so it is also a symbol of advancement in life through courage, strength and patience.

Traditional *kakejiku* scrolls
These scrolls are hung in the tokonuma alcove in a traditional Japanese room. Designs include calligraphy as well as pictorial subjects, sometimes combined. Rubbings of Buddhist texts from ancient carvings are sometimes mounted as scrolls too, while kakejiku used for tea ceremony may have a short poem, phrase or a single word – the kanji on this scroll is 'Bu', the first syllable of Buddha. In addition to watercolours on paper or silk, sumi-e (ink pictures) may be monochrome designs in ink.

Fig 1 Koi template (actual size): trace or photocopy the diagram, and then flip the tracing over to trace a mirror image koi. The picture opposite shows the lower fish in detail.

Kimono Wall Hanging

This wall hanging is an opportunity to try out various sashiko techniques in one piece and combine them with simple patchwork and appliqué. The little kimono is stitched in outline, with individual *shippō* (seven treasures) crests across the shoulders, a crane over the centre back and the *komezashi* (rice stitch) variation spanning the full width. Hexagonal appliqués use striped *tsumugi* cotton to border the sashiko designs, repeating *shippō* along with a single *asanoha* (hemp leaf), *minka* (farmhouse) motif and hexagonal variations of *masuzashi* (square measure) and *hanabishizashi*. The finished panel has a striped border, with optional extra wadding (batting) and hand quilting following the sashiko outlines.

The little kimono design used in the wall hanging is based on the tiny garments used for the *miyamairi* ceremony, the Shinto equivalent of a christening, when babies are taken to the local shrine to be blessed. These kimono are usually very decorative, with a large centre back motif and plenty of lucky images.

Technique Taster

Try out the sashiko in the hexagon patches by making these coasters. Any of the hexagon motifs could be used and I chose the farmhouse and the *hanabishizashi* design. See instructions overleaf. Other sashiko designs could be adapted to the hexagonal format.

Baby boys' *miyamairi*
kimono are usually black
or blue but girls' kimono
are often more colourful
– red, orange, pink or
green. The motifs used
on this wall hanging are
appropriate for boys and
girls. Instructions for the
hanging are on page 114.

Coasters

Sashiko patterns used: *hanabishizashi* (flower diamond stitch) variation and *minka* (farmhouse) motif

Finished size: 3¾in (9.5cm) wide

You will need
(for two coasters)

- Two scraps of sashiko fabric, large enough for the hexagon pattern
- Scraps of striped *tsumugi* or similar cotton, for the border strips
- Two backing fabric pieces 4¼in x 4in (10.8cm x 10.2cm)
- Fine sashiko thread in cream
- Sewing thread
- Basic sewing and marking kit

1 Making the patchwork:

Assemble the patchwork first. Trace or photocopy the patchwork templates in **Fig 1** below (seam allowances are included). For each design, cut one hexagon (A) from the sashiko fabric. Cut three small pieces (B) and three longer pieces (C). Using ¼in (6mm) seams throughout, pin and machine sew three B pieces to the centre hexagon and press seams outwards. Pin and sew the longer C pieces and press outwards.

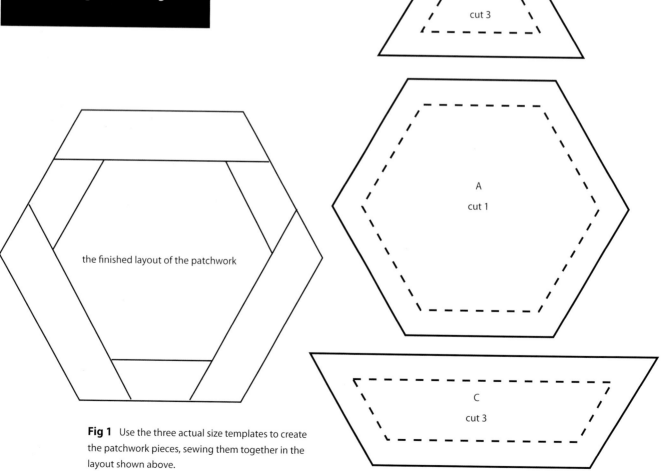

B
cut 3

A
cut 1

C
cut 3

the finished layout of the patchwork

Fig 1 Use the three actual size templates to create the patchwork pieces, sewing them together in the layout shown above.

2 Marking the sashiko:

For the *hanabishizashi* (flower diamond stitch) variation, mark lines linking the corners of the hexagon to the centre and stitch the pattern following **Fig 2**.

For the *minka* (farmhouse) motif, trace the template given in **Fig 3** and transfer it using Chaco paper (page 21) or a lightbox.

3 Stitching the sashiko:

Stitch *hanabishizashi* by stitching the first row forming the first two 'petals' along the centre vertical line, shown in red on the orange shaded background, and build up the pattern on either side of this row, with the gaps between the stitches in each petal about half the length of the stitch and a longer gap at the end of each petal. Strand the thread across the back in the longer gaps between stitches (see page 27). Repeat for the other two diagonal sections.

Stitch the farmhouse motif working around the design, across the bottom line, then across the house, up and down the 'posts', completing roof and 'cloud' lines. Press both sashiko pieces when complete.

Fig 2 *hanabishizashi* (flower diamond stitch) variation: mark the pattern following the diagram.

4 Assembling the coasters:

Pin one coaster right sides together with a piece of backing fabric and sew around five sides with a 1/4in (6mm) seam allowance, using the striped fabric as a guide. Trim the backing to match the edge of the hexagon all round. Trim off corners within the seam allowance, but do not cut right up to the stitches – to about 1/8in (3mm). Ease the corners out so they are sharp. Turn the coaster right side out through the unsewn gap. Turn the gap edges under 1/4in (6mm) and slipstitch closed. Press to finish.

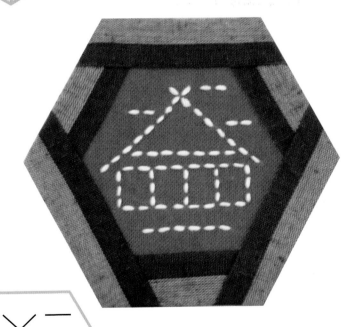

Idea
Try stitching other sashiko patterns in a hexagon format, adapting the design to fit the shape, by having six rather than four divisions, such as a six-segment version of *shippō*.

Fig 3 *minka* (farmhouse) motif: use this actual size template to mark the house pattern.

113

Kimono Hanging

Sashiko patterns used: *shippō* (seven treasures), *komezashi* (rice stitch) variation, *asanoha* (hemp leaf), *minka* (farmhouse) motif, *masuzashi* (square measure) variation and *hanabishizashi* (flower diamond stitch) variation

Finished size: 35½in x 33½in (90.2cm x 85.1cm)

You will need

- Sashiko fabric 32in x 28in (81.3cm x 71.1cm)
- Striped *tsumugi* or similar cotton for border:
  two strips 36in x 3½in (91.4cm x 8.9cm)
  two strips 28in x 3½in (71.1cm x 8.9cm)
- Scraps of striped *tsumugi* or similar cotton for hexagon border strips
- Five scraps of sashiko fabric, large enough for hexagon pattern (Fig 1 page 112)
- Backing fabric 36in x 34in (91.4cm x 86.4cm)
- 2oz wadding (batting) 36in x 34in (91.4cm x 86.4cm) (optional)
- Plain cotton 33½in x 8in (85.1cm x 20.3cm), for hanging sleeve
- Fine sashiko thread in cream, yellow ochre and light green and medium in shaded blues
- Sewing thread
- Basic sewing and marking kit

Tip
Mark parallel identical curves easily with a ruler: with the ruler parallel to the vertical lines, measure 3in (7.6cm), 1in (2.5cm), 1in and 1in and mark a dot at these points. Work across the curve, marking dots every ½in (1.3cm) across the panel. Then simply join the dots to create identical curves.

1 **Making the appliqués:**
Make five patchwork hexagons, following the coaster instructions in step 1 on page 112. Mark and stitch the *hanabishizashi* and *minka* appliqués following the coaster instructions in steps 2 and 3 on page 113. Mark the *shippō*, *asanoha* and *masuzashi* variations as shown and described opposite in **Fig 1**, **Fig 2** and **Fig 3**. Press each finished piece. Turn under ¼in (6mm) all round and press.

2 **Marking the centre panel:**
Zigzag or overlock the panel before you begin. Mark a 30in x 26in (76.2cm x 66cm) rectangle on the 32in x 28in (81.3cm x 71.1cm) sashiko fabric piece. Mark a temporary line down the exact centre. Mark the design as shown in **Fig 4** overleaf, starting with the horizontal shoulder line, the vertical lines on either side of the kimono and the bottom of the sleeves. Mark the angled front panels by drawing the bottom line first, drawing the other line at a 90-degree corner angle. The *shippō* motifs at the top are centred on the back and the sleeves and 1½in (3.8cm) down from the shoulder line. The collar (top) is centred on the back, so measure 2in (5cm) and 1½in (3.8cm) on either side of the temporary centre line. Mark the first wavy line freehand, slightly above the midpoint of the sleeves. Mark the other four lines parallel to this, at 3in (7.6cm) and then 1in (2.5cm) intervals.

Minka hexagon – see coaster instructions, steps 2 and 3 on page 113.

Hanabishizashi hexagon – see coaster instructions, steps 2 and 3 on page 113.

Fig 1 Shippō: mark a horizontal and vertical line through the centre of the fabric hexagon. Using a 2in (5cm) diameter circle template, mark the circle and then the four quarter circles. Stitch the pattern.

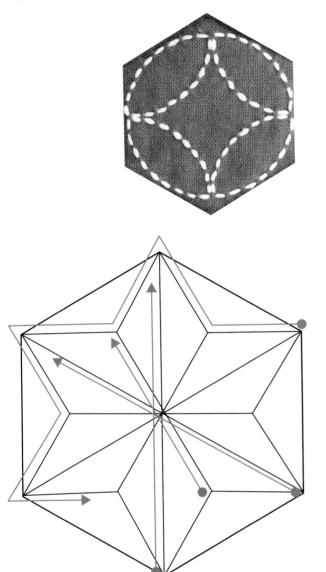

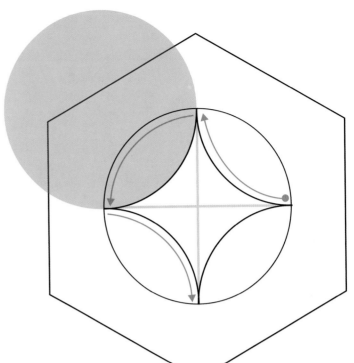

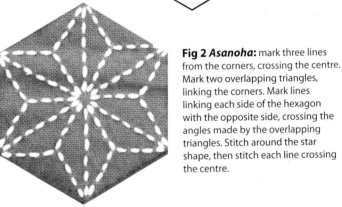

Fig 2 Asanoha: mark three lines from the corners, crossing the centre. Mark two overlapping triangles, linking the corners. Mark lines linking each side of the hexagon with the opposite side, crossing the angles made by the overlapping triangles. Stitch around the star shape, then stitch each line crossing the centre.

Fig 3 Masuzashi: working inwards from the edge of the hexagon, mark lines ¼in (6mm) apart, parallel to the edges, and crossing the ends of adjacent lines. Stitch the sashiko, working around the outer set of lines first, crossing the corners by one stitch, and stranding across the back to the next line, in the same sequence used for the square masuzashi in Fig 3 on page 101.

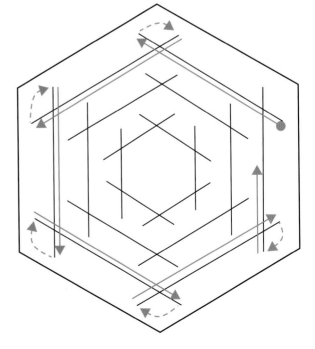

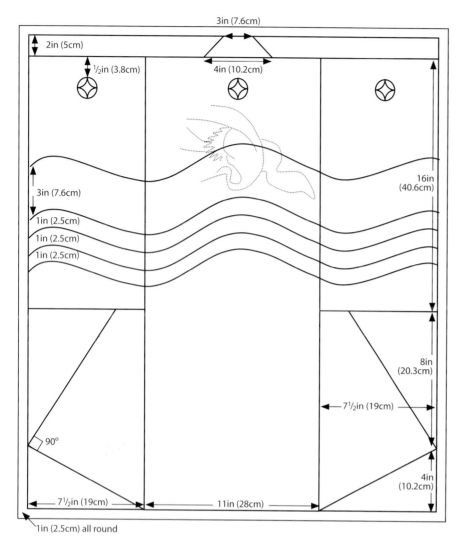

Fig 4 Marking out the centre panel

3in (7.6cm)

2in (5cm)

½in (3.8cm)

4in (10.2cm)

16in (40.6cm)

3in (7.6cm)

1in (2.5cm)

1in (2.5cm)

1in (2.5cm)

8in (20.3cm)

7½in (19cm)

90°

4in (10.2cm)

7½in (19cm)

11in (28cm)

1in (2.5cm) all round

3 Trace or photocopy the crane pattern from **Fig 5** on page 118. Using either the Chaco paper method on page 21 or a lightbox, trace the pattern on to the centre back of the 'kimono', lining it up by eye.

4 ## Stitching the appliqué:

Arrange the appliqué motifs using the photograph opposite as a guide. Pin and tack the appliqués to the sashiko panel and then hand sew them with small, neat stitches. Work with the edge of the appliqué towards you. Bring the needle up through the sashiko fabric and edge of the appliqué, then down through the sashiko fabric, keeping the stitch at right angles to the edge and about 1/16in (2mm) apart.

5 ## Stitching the sashiko:

Using the cream thread, begin by stitching the kimono outlines, with single lines of sashiko stitches. Stitch the *shippō* motifs, following Fig 1 and its instructions. Stitch the crane, working around the motif and adding details by stitching up and down the feathers. Stitch a paired line of sashiko stitches along each curve, using yellow ochre thread for the lines on either side of the widest curved band. When stitching this paired line, stitch the first row of stitches on the marked line, making sure the gap is about half the length of the stitch. Stitch the second row close to the first, staggering the stitches so that the new stitches overlap the gaps.

Yellow ochre and shaded blue threads keep the *komezashi* variation from overwhelming the crane, which is stitched in cream.

6 Mark and stitch the *komezashi* variation following Fig 4 and its instructions on page 36. Mark a 1in (2.5cm) grid all over the 3in curved band. Stitch the pattern using the medium shaded blue sashiko thread.

7 Making the patchwork:

Press the finished sashiko panel. Remove the tacking stitches from the appliqué pieces, turn the panel over and carefully trim away the backing fabric behind the appliqués, leaving at least a ¼in (6mm) of the backing fabric inside the appliqué stitch line. Pin the top and bottom striped border strips to the centre panel and machine sew with a ¼in (6mm) seam allowance. Press seams towards the border strips. Repeat for the side border panels.

Tip
Cotton and cotton/polyester blend wadding (batting) is less likely to 'beard' or shed through the sashiko fabric. Blended wadding is also available in black – ideal for use behind dark sashiko fabric.

8 Making up the wall hanging:

If using wadding and intending to quilt the wall hanging, assemble the layers as follows. Lay the wadding flat and smooth. Lay the backing fabric right side up on the wadding and tack the two layers together, at about 4in (10.2cm) intervals, horizontally and vertically. Place the patchwork panel right sides together with the backing panel and pin all round. Machine sew wadding, backing and panel together around the edges with a ¼in (6mm) seam allowance, leaving an 8in (20.3cm) gap in the centre of the lower edge. Trim off the corners within the seam allowance but do not cut right up to the stitches – to about ⅛in (3mm) is fine. Turn the hanging over so the wadding is on top and carefully trim away excess wadding within the seam allowance. Turn the hanging right way out through the unsewn gap, easing out the corners. Turn under the raw edges at the bottom and slipstitch the gap.

If you are *not* using wadding, make up the hanging as follows. Place the front panel and backing fabric right sides together and pin all round. Machine sew with a ¼in (6mm) seam allowance, leaving an 8in (20.3cm) gap in the centre of the lower edge. Trim off the corners within the seam allowance but do not cut right

The patchwork borders sewn to the main panel.

up to the stitches – to about ⅛in (3mm). Turn the hanging out through the unsewn gap and ease out corners so they are sharp. Lay the hanging flat and smooth. Turn under the raw edges at the bottom and slipstitch the gap. From the back, sew right around the hanging, about ⅛in (3mm) from the edge, with small, neat hand stitches through backing and seam allowances only, to keep the backing in place.

9 Optional extra quilting:

Quilt next to the sashiko line, on the outside of the motif, but without going over the sashiko stitches, matching your thread closely to the fabric colour. Quilt around or along: the kimono outline; the vertical lines and the diagonal kimono front panel sections; the *shippō* circles, crane and appliqués individually; the hexagons inside the appliqués; the top, centre and lower horizontal curved lines and the inside edge of the striped border.

10 Making a hanging sleeve:

To finish the hanging follow step 8 on page 87 to make a hanging sleeve.

Idea

I hand quilted the wall hanging, but it can also be machine quilted. Adding wadding and extra quilting to finished sashiko gives this panel additional dimension and body. Machine quilting next to the sashiko outline gives a more defined line than hand quilting and can be seen on the single Koi panel in the Inspiration Gallery on page 120.

Fig 5 Crane template (actual size)
– trace or photocopy

Sashiko Inspirations

Miyamairi kimono

Decorated with auspicious motifs, these kimono are a good size for a wall display. Typical motifs include, tsuru (crane), tsuru kame (crane and turtle) and matsu (pine), for wishes for a long life, while noshi (decorative bundle of dried abalone) and sensu (folding fan) are for increase and prosperity. Takarazukushi, the collection of treasures, may be depicted as individual items, as in the hexagons on this boy's kimono, or on a treasure ship, bringing good fortune and prosperity. Animals associated with strength, such as tigers, lions, hawks and koi also feature on boy's miyamairi kimono, sometimes with samurai motifs, such as armour. Girl's designs include butterflies, temari (a decorative embroidered ball), tsuzumi (hand drum) and flowers. Like adult's formal kimono, these also have five family crests across the shoulders, three across the back. Unisex miyamairi kimono do not exist, so use blue and black colour schemes for a boy's wall hanging and orange, red, pink or green for a girl's.

Kikkō designs

Hexagons are an abstract representation of turtle or tortoise shell, so they also represent longevity. Early examples of this design date from the 9th century. Hexagons filled with quatrefoil karabana (Chinese flowers) became popular about 1,000 years ago and are used for many textiles today, including karaori (Chinese weave) brocade, used for Nō costumes and obi. Larger hexagons may be filled with flowers or landscapes, like the komon (small pattern) kimono detail shown above and the indigo katazome sample on page 95. Both were stencil dyed. Other hexagon patterns include stacked hexagons and overlapping hexagons. The tiny hishizashi kikkō on page 93 is another version.

Inspiration Gallery

I've used sashiko on all the quilts and cushions in this gallery, combining sashiko with patchwork and appliqué in an innovative way, adding texture and colour or creating new sashiko patterns or variations from a traditional design. Using sashiko in your original work will help to keep the tradition alive and evolving for centuries to come.

A single image from the Koi scroll on page 103 is framed with Japanese patchwork fabric for this small wall hanging. Polyester wadding (batting), added after the sashiko was completed, and machine quilting around the koi and inside the border gives the piece extra depth. The traditional indigo and white colour scheme makes this piece feel calm and fresh.
The wall hanging measures 13in x 15$\frac{1}{2}$in (33cm x 39.4cm).

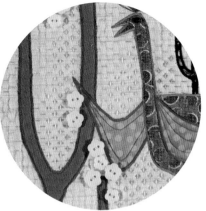

Sashiko doesn't have to be restricted to Japanese themed projects. *Yokogushi* and *jūjizashi* (both on page 91) *hitomezashi* (one stitch sashiko) stitching adds texture and subtle colour to the background of this machine appliquéd wall hanging, stitched through a thin cotton wadding (batting). 'Pink Paradise Birdsong' was inspired by 1950s furnishing fabrics, Constance Howard's embroidery designs and 1960s children's TV characters. It was awarded first place in Quilt Art at The Great Northern Quilt Show (UK), 2005, and won awards for Computer-aided Design and Judge's Choice.
The wall hanging measures 31in x 21in (78.7cm x 53.3cm).

Mōyozashi adapts well to big stitch quilting. 'Time and Again' features a square in a square pattern adapted from *masuzashi* (page 101), with a curved flame motif. Both designs, stitched with a single hand-dyed thread, follow the patchwork background, which borders 2in (5cm) squares of vintage kimono scraps with contemporary batiks, accented with appliqué *sakura* (cherry blossoms) made from hand-dyed cotton. The wadding is dark polyester. It won a Judges Merit award at the National Quilting Championships (UK), 2001. The piece measures 60in x 40in (152.5cm x 101.6cm).

Shippō (seven treasures) variations as big stitch quilting combine with patchwork and appliqué on the '99 Treasures' quilt and 'Takara' (treasures) cushion. Sewing *shippō* over appliqué squares echoes the *shippō* variation on page 84, with the appliqué circle replacing the inner sashiko circle. Only half the *shippō* wavy line is stitched on the quilt's white squares. Polyester wadding (batting) gives a puffy effect. I used a single strand of metallic gold thread to quilt the cushion and hand-dyed cotton for the quilt. The quilt won second place in Cot (crib) Quilts at Quilts UK, 2003. The quilt is 52in x 44in (132cm x 111.8cm) and the cushion is 17½in (44.5cm) square.

Individual leaf and flower motifs are quick and easy to stitch, so simple sets of coasters and placemats like these make ideal gift projects. Motifs are plum and bamboo (page 59), *momiji* (maple, page 34), *sakura* (cherry blossom page 36) and *kiku* (chrysanthemum, page 105). Plain cream and shaded sashiko threads are used to colour co-ordinate the sets. Placemats are 10¾ x 12¾in (27.3 x 32.4cm) and coasters are 3½in (8.9cm) square.

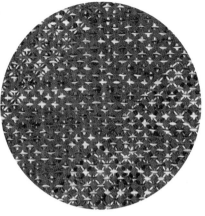

Hitomezashi patterns *yokogushi* (horizontal rows), *jūjizashi* ('10' cross stitch), *kikkōzashi* (tortoiseshell stitch) and *komezashi* (rice stitch) variations look ultra modern stitched in shaded brown sashiko thread on this cushion (see Kiku Panel instructions on pages 91 and 93 for all these stitches). The pattern arrangement is based on traditional sashiko *donza* (work coats) worn by fishermen from Awaji island, which were often stitched as virtuoso samplers and worn for festivals and special occasions. The Awaji cushion measures 18in (45.7cm) square.

All-over sashiko patterns look good stitched over a patchwork of squares and rectangles, as shown here with *asanoha* (hemp leaf). The patchwork design is adapted from *shimacho* ('stripe book') scrapbook pages, made as reference books by weavers. It looks random but, like *shimacho*, the larger pieces show off more elaborate *kasuri* (ikat) weaves while small pieces have small patterns. The cushion mixes old and new fabrics. The sashiko is quilted through three layers, with thin cotton wadding and a doubled strand of fine sashiko thread. The cushion is 21in (53.3cm) square.

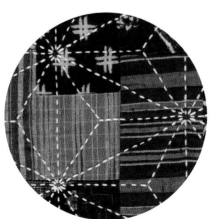

123

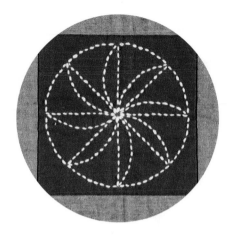

This patchwork and sashiko sampler combines five sashiko motifs from Sakata, Shonai, with easy patchwork, including a faux patchwork fabric giving the illusion of extra ranru (tatter cloth) piecing. The motifs include two *shippō* (seven treasures) variations (page 86), *raimon* (spiral, page 101) and a triangular version of *raimon*. The centre motif is a design I learned from the late Chieko Hori, a sashiko expert from Yuza-machi. A simple patchwork setting is a great way to combine sashiko sample squares and could be adapted for a larger group project. The Sakata sampler measures 23½in (59.7cm) square.

'Zen – Garden from the Tea House' was inspired by the Kyoto-style tea room at the Dewa Yushinkan pavilion, Sakata City in Japan. Japanese architecture is a great source of designs, like the circular window. An appliquéd tea bowl awaits the guest. Each wall panel has a *mōyozashi* design, including *asanoha* (hemp leaf, page 98), *nowaki* (page 87) and two patterns from my first sashiko book (*The Ultimate Sashiko Sourcebook*, D&C, 2005), quilted in a single hand-dyed thread through a thin polyester wadding (batting). Other big stitch quilting suggests the raked gravel garden seen through the low doorway and ridges on the *tatami* mat and bamboo wall panel. The maple leaves are appliquéd using the same template as the sashiko motif on page 34. This quilt and the one opposite were made for an exhibition in Yamagata City in 2001 and have been exhibited several times in Japan. The quilt measures 37in x 25in (94cm x 63.5cm).

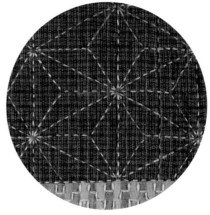

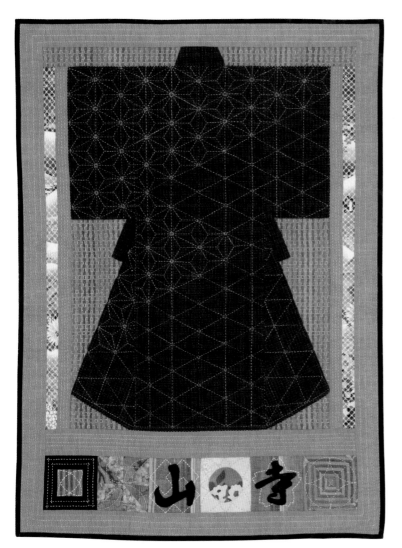

The kimono shape makes a good background for all over sashiko and I've used it here to show the two main stages for stitching *asanoha* (hemp leaf, page 98). *Komezashi* (rice stitch, page 91) stitched with a single fine thread creates a lattice effect over landscape fabric strips on either side of the kimono. The background is stitched with *kakinohanazashi* (persimmon flower stitch, from my first sashiko book) lined up on striped cotton, but *hishizashi* (page 46) would work just as well. The squares include *masuzashi* (page 101) around a patchwork square, *shippō* variations (pages 84 and 35) and a *sakura* (cherry blossom) outline (page 36). The appliquéd *kanji* characters are *yama* (mountain) and *tera* (temple), which combine to read 'Yamadera', the famous Rishakuji Buddhist temple near Yamagata City in Japan. Colours represent autumn at the temple and I quilted the whole piece through very thin cotton wadding (batting). The quilt measures 39in x 27in (99cm x 68.6cm).

These tranquil leaves remind me of a graceful weeping willow and were adapted from a 1960s kimono design. The leaf shapes overlap here and there like *shippō* (seven treasures) circles. The repeated vertical line, the simple shapes and the use of just two threads, one plain and one shaded, keep the design fresh and modern.
The cushion is 18in (45.7cm) square.

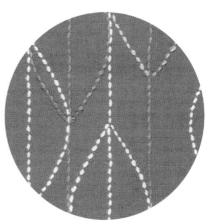

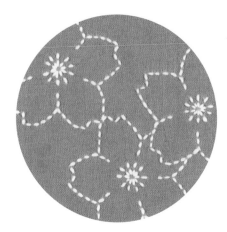

A large triangle square is an easy way to combine a large-scale patchwork print with sashiko fabric. This Japanese print was too interesting to cut into small pieces, so I used the *sakura* (cherry blossom) sashiko motif (page 36) to emphasize the blossoms in the print. It was easy to mark by making a cardboard sakura template, so I could overlap the motifs for a natural effect. The cushion is 16½in (42cm) square.

About the author

Susan Briscoe writes and designs for patchwork and quilting magazines, and teaches patchwork and sashiko quilting. She was first introduced to sashiko in the early 1990s while teaching English in northern Japan and on a return visit learned the technique from local sashiko experts. In 2003 she brought an exhibition of historic and contemporary sashiko pieces to the UK's Festival of Quilts, which ultimately led in 2005 to the creation of her best-selling book for David & Charles, *The Ultimate Sashiko Sourcebook*.

Susan has published two additional books so far for David & Charles - *21 Terrific Patchwork Bags* in 2003 and *21 Sensational Patchwork Bags* in 2006.

Suppliers

High-street stores are great sources of ideas for items to display your sashiko projects – keep your eyes open and your creative radar will soon spot some gems. In Japan, sashiko supplies are sold in virtually every handicraft or sewing store

UK

Susan Briscoe Designs
Yamadera, 4 Mount Zion, Brymbo, Wrexham LL11 5NB
Email: susan@briscoedesigns.freeserve.co.uk
www.susanbriscoe.co.uk
For vintage Japanese textiles, kits and patterns (mail order only)

Designs available as kits from Euro Japan Links Limited (see contact details, right): Koi panel (page 120), Takara cushion (page 122), placemats and coasters (page 122), Awaji cushion (page 123), Sakata sampler (page 124) and cushions (pages 125 and 126). Please check for availability. Colours and fabrics may vary. 'Time and Again' (page 121), '99 Treasures' (page 122), and Shimacho cushion (page 123) are available as patterns from Susan Briscoe Designs (see above).

The Cotton Patch
1285 Stratford Road, Hall Green, Birmingham West Midlands B28 9AJ
Tel: 0121 7022840
Email: mailorder@cottonpatch.net
www.cottonpatch.co.uk
For quilters' rulers, fabric markers and quilting supplies (webstore, mail order and shop)

Euro Japan Links Ltd
32 Nant Road, Childs Hill, London NW2 2AT
Tel: 020 8201 9324
Email: eurojpn@aol.com
www.eurojapanlinks.com
For Japanese textiles and sashiko supplies (mail order only)

USA

The Shibori Dragon
11124 Gravelly Lake Drive SW, Lakewood WA 98499
Tel: (253) 582-7455
Fax: (253) 512-2323
Email: shiboridragon@juno.com
www.shiboridragon.com
For Japanese textiles and sashiko supplies (webstore and mail order)

Japan

Kimono Flea Market Ichiroya
Asia-Shoji Bldg. 301, 1841-1 Nishi 1 chome Wakamatsu cho Tondabayashi, Osaka 584-0025
email: info@ichiroya.com
www.ichiroya.com
For vintage textiles, sashiko and Japanese antiques (webstore and mail order)

Acknowledgments

I would like to thank the following people for their help and support in making this book: Reiko Domon and Chie Ikeda for sashiko advice and help; my friends at Peaceful Heart Quilt Group, Yuza-machi, Japan; the Director of Chido Museum Mr Tadahisa Sakai and Miss Kayo Sakai; Keiko Hori, for sharing her family's garden (photo on page 107); Mary and Shiro Tamakoshi (Euro Japan Links Limited); all my friends in Japan; my family and friends in the UK; and finally all the team at David & Charles, who helped me turn an inspiration into a book.

Index